the WORLD according to God

a biblical view of culture, work, science, sex & everything else

Greg Johnson

InterVarsity Press
Downers Grove, Illinois

InterVarsity Press
P.O. Box 1400, Downers Grove, IL 60515-1426
World Wide Web: www.ivpress.com
E-mail: mail@ivpress.com

InterVarsity Press® is the book-publishing division of InterVarsity Christian Fellowship/USA®, a student movement active on campus at hundreds of universities, colleges and schools of nursing in the
United States of America, and a member movement of the International Fellowship of Evangelical
Students. For information about local and regional activities, write Public Relations Dept., InterVarsity Christian Fellowship/USA, 6400 Schroeder Rd., P.O. Box 7895, Madison, WI 53707-7895, or visit
the IVCF website at <www.ivcf.org>.

Cover and title page illustrations:
  Pears, newspaper, gloves, mouse and globe: RubberBall Production
  Flower: Eyewire

ISBN 0-8308-2335-2

Printed in the United States of America ∞

Library of Congress Cataloging-in-Publication Data

Johnson, Gregory, 1972-
    The world according to God: a biblical view of culture, work, science, sex &
everything else / Gregory Johnson.
        p. cm.
    Includes bibliographical references.
    ISBN 0-8308-2335-2 (pbk.: alk. paper)
    1. Christian life—Biblical teaching. I. Title.
    BS2545.C48 J65 2002
    230'.04624—dc21   2001051940

P	17	16	15	14	13	12	11	10	9	8	7	6	5	4	3	2	1
Y	15	14	13	12	11	10	09	08	07	06	05	04	03	02			

Contents

Choose Your Own ~~Adventure~~ Introduction

Introduction #1
For Academics Who Like Big Words like *Metanarrative*

I always had trouble narrowing paper topics when I was a student. I guess it makes sense that my first book is about *everything*. Of course, I did manage to narrow the topic to everything *according to God.* That's progress.

Some in the academic world will immediately dismiss this book just because of its title. They'll say it's *presumptuous* because it claims to present God's perspective. I'm not so concerned about secular academics who think we can't know what God thinks about life, but I'm terrified when supposedly Christian scholars hesitate to say, "God says so." We've caved into a relativistic postmodern worldview that overqualifies every statement to the point that our caution looks a lot like what Christians once called unbelief.

The academic world doesn't like clear statements. Today it's not unthinkable that an evangelical scholar might say something like this:

> *For me personally, from my limited perspective, I think it would appear to me—if I'm not mistaken about this—that there's one primary Savior in the*

Bible, at least according to my faith tradition, within my circle of meaning,
assuming a premodern metanarrative and a faith-based discourse as we
tend to do, I think.

Weasels.

There's a difference between being aware of your limitations and being a coward. We used to just say, "Jesus is the only Savior." It's a clear, concise statement, powerful in its simplicity. Besides, God says so (Acts 4:12).

Of course, the use of a prooftext like the one above brings another charge to bolster the first. Some academics will accuse this poor little book of being *naive* because its author thinks we can actually understand much of the text of the Bible, given the right use of means. How dare I simply quote or reference the Bible as if it's self-explanatory? These critics assume that the Bible is so conditioned by cultural contexts that specific texts don't really speak to us today.

I certainly hope I've done my work in the original languages, checked out commentaries, taken genre changes into account, and considered literary, cultural, linguistic, historical, biblical-theological, systematic and canonical contexts. But once all that work has been done—and it shouldn't be flaunted in a popular-level book—the fact remains that when God says so, God says so (Acts 4:12). I dare not ignore explicit texts and their explicit meanings and significance in the name of affirming "broad themes" from Scripture. The Bible really does speak today—*specifically.*

When I look through much of the recent theological literature published in evangelical circles, I quickly become discouraged. Even where nothing false is being said, there's so very little Scripture in it. Though some may call me a fire-breathing fundamentalist for it, I have to say that I've had enough of discourses, communities, constructions and metanarratives. The postmodern categories of academia bore me. The churches need bread from heaven. They need more Bible.

The direction of postmodern scholarship has been to introduce ambiguity into human discourse, and this skepticism has infected many supposedly Christian institutions. I remember one professor at an evangelical Bible college not long ago getting very upset with me for calling the Bible "God's word" and "communication from God." "It's just a construction," he insisted, his face red with anger.

Just a construction? The Scriptures call themselves the word of God (Mk 7:13), the Law of God (Neh 8:8), the very words of God (Rom 3:2), the law of the LORD (2 Chron 17:9), the word of truth (2 Tim 2:15), the sword of the Spirit (Eph 6:17), the breath of God (2 Tim 3:16). Sure, the Scriptures are a discourse—but an objective, true and binding discourse of discourses whose author-behind-the-authors is God.

In the 1970s, a generation of biblical Christians saw a great deal of conflict (particularly in North America) over the doctrine of the Bible's inerrancy—its total trustworthiness in historical as well as theological matters. By the middle of the 1980s, however, flower power had gone, disco was out, and a consensus had arisen among conservative Christians that the Bible was indeed God's inerrant word.

But if the battle for the Bible's inerrancy is over—and I'm not convinced it is—then the battle for both the perspicuity and sufficiency of the Bible (the clarity and unique authority of its central teachings) is just heating up. We need to decide whether we can really know what God is saying in the Scriptures, and if so, whether it's everything we need for life and godliness.

This is the evangelical context into which I have written. I believe that the God of Abraham, Isaac and Jacob created everything that exists, and that all the various spheres of life are established by him for his glory and our good. I believe that Jesus Christ holds all authority on earth and that his gospel brings redemptive power into every sphere of life on earth. I believe that Christ exercises his lordship over his world through the Scriptures, which have the power to change even the hardest of hearts. It changed and is changing mine.

Don't misunderstand me. This book is *not* a volley in the coming battle over the Bible. I hate conflict and dread the day when churches are split because trendy evangelicals have abandoned the truth in the name of being inclusive or pluralistic. But I do hope God uses this book to display the power of his Word in the lives of his people. Such is the power of classical biblical Christian theology.[1]

We desperately need the Scriptures. Sure I draw from more than bare biblical exegesis—the Reformation doctrine of *sola scriptura* doesn't mean we approach the Bible in a vacuum. The Bible alone has the authority to bind the conscience, but the Bible should be read within the context of two thousand years of Christian thought. We aren't the first generation to read the Bible, and we're naive if we refuse to gain from the work of those believers who have gone before us. God has given his church teachers in the past, just as he does today. Nothing in this book is original. And in an age when a book has to be about constructions of metanarratives within communities of discourse, I find that kind of refreshing.

Think about that—what the Bible says about everyday life, without postmodern window-dressing.

Wow.

I'll even say it backwards. Wow.

My spiritual journey has been diverse. I attended a humanistic university—humanistic in both the good sense and the bad sense. But I encountered a merciful God though the ministry of Campus Crusade for Christ. I learned that the Bible was the living voice of God. I went from there to a Reformed seminary in the Puritan tradition, and I came to understand more than ever the character of the God we serve. And though my doctoral studies took me to a Roman Catholic university, I've found no greater goal than that expressed by the Protestant Reformers of the sixteenth century: *Soli Deo gloria*. To God alone be the glory.

This God has given us the many spheres of life as realms of his glory. We don't so much give all of life to God as we *receive all of life from God*. He is the fount of every blessing; we are the parched earth awaiting his living waters. He is the Creator; we are the creatures. He is the giver

---

[1]Don't doubt that this is a work of theology. Sure, it's written for a popular audience; think of it as theology *incognito*—living biblical truth for real people of God. Just don't tell anyone it's theology—at least not until they've finished chapter one.

of good gifts; we are the recipients. "Every good and perfect gift is from above, coming down from the Father of the heavenly lights, who does not change like shifting shadows" (Jas 1:17).

The doctrine of creation isn't just what we fight evolutionists with; it's the context within which we live out our daily existence. God's blessings are not limited to our devotional times, ministries and worship services. All of life—work, art, people, relationships, sexuality, communication, the sciences and education, *everything*—is related to the God who is sovereign over it. Every sphere of life is a gift from God. And every corner of our lives is the object of Christ's healing, saving, restoring power.

"I am the vine; you are the branches," Jesus said, "If a man remains in me and I in him, he will bear much fruit; apart from me you can do nothing" (Jn 15:5). When the Father awakens us by his sovereign Spirit, we draw from Christ's life the resurrection power that enables us to love God's world, even as we await its full restoration at the end of the age.

Introduction #2

For Normal People (I Wrote This Book for *You!*)

We too easily settle for a mediocre life when God gives us a whole world and says, "See, this is for you!" (That's a very rough paraphrase of Genesis 1:28.) In too many churches sinners are called to faith in Jesus but never taught what Jesus says about their everyday lives. God tells us about a lot more than forgiveness, quiet times and being good.

As you read this book, I'm confident God will press his imprint into every area of your life. God isn't just calling you to give 100 percent of your life to him. It's better than that. *He's going to give 100 percent of your life to you.* Everything you do will be a calling from your Father; all the hats you wear in life will be designed by him. How's that for a famous label?

You'll get your sex life from God, your job from God, your athlete's foot from God (sorry) and your new wallpaper from God. I'm not joking—the Bible says that every bit of this and more comes from God the Creator. Better than that, it's all *good* if you know how to receive it. Want to know the details? Keep reading.

Does focusing on life in this world sidetrack Christians from what's really important? Hardly. Jesus' Great Commission involves "teaching them to obey everything I have commanded" (Mt 28:18-20). When we consider that this Jesus was the same Lord who spoke in the Old Testament, that's a whopper of a lot of commands—more than you can shake a rod and staff at. But his commands come with the promise that he'll be our God and we'll be his people. God not only gives you the world, he gives you himself. What more could you ask for?

There's life-changing, world-shaking, idol-smashing power in the Word of God. We resign ourselves too quickly to a dreary walk with God revolving around a handful of trite religious truisms and a load of guilt and shame at not being good little Christian men and women. That's not the life God promises us.

I'm convinced that Christian clichés will never satisfy the soul. We need spiritually hearty meals loaded with the whole counsel of God, the kind of solid food that turns our worlds upside down for Jesus Christ. We don't need someone else's perspective on life or another shallow call to do better. We need a vision bigger than ourselves, the big picture, God 24-7. The joy of a Godward life awaits us when we see the entire world according to God.

1

MORE THAN SAVED

Everything According to God

"In the beginning . . ."
GENESIS 1:1

One popular Bible teacher has complained that Christians get too involved in the affairs of this world. He asks, "Why polish the brass if the ship's sinking?" Since this present world is passing away, why invest our time and energy in things like the arts, accounting, politics, relationships, education or scientific advancement? Shouldn't we devote all our effort to preaching the gospel? Since no one can be saved apart from faith in Jesus aren't we wasting precious time polishing the world's brass when the ship is going down?

It's Time to Polish the Brass

I remember struggling through this question in college. I'd worked untold hours in the architecture studio, cutting out little bits of balsa wood, neatly fitting them together, falling asleep over vellum drawings, hoping I wouldn't drool and ruin them. But each day I'd spend only half an hour praying and reading my Bible. I sensed the imbalance. Hours and hours in the architecture studio, thirty minutes in the Bible. Was I wasting my time? Did God want me to push the Villa Medici aside and spend the entire day reading my Bible and praying, venturing out only to tell others about Jesus? Is that why Jesus came?

Throughout my college years this same issue resurfaced. I was deeply aware of the abortion controversy in those days and wanted to help the pro-life cause. I read about one third of American babies being aborted, and so I gave myself to increasing public awareness about the humanity of unborn children.

I distributed leaflets, sponsored public speakers and videos, met with lawmakers, and wrote for the student papers. But again and again well-meaning Christians told me I was wasting my time—only preaching the gospel would do any eternal good. You can imagine the confusion and guilt a skinny nineteen year old feels when other Christians criticize him for trying to help "this world." Deep in my heart I struggled. Why did God put me on this earth?

I think a lot of us struggle over the eternal value of our "secular" lives. We long for wholeness. We see the different areas of our lives shooting off into different directions. On the one hand you're an accountant, on the other a Christian. But you long to be a Christian accountant. Does knowing God mean retreating into our prayer closets or advancing our prayer closets into the workplace and culture? To discover what God wants us doing and why, we need to look back to creation and the pattern of life God gave us then.

Go Back to Creation

If I want to know what a toaster is supposed to do, I ask why it was created. It was created to make toast. If I want to know what a DVD player should do, I have to look at its creation. It was made to play digital videodisks. What if I try to make toast in a DVD player? Messy. Why the device was made dictates what it should do.

Similarly, if we want to know what God wants us to do, we should ask why he created us. Nowhere can we find a clearer answer than in the Bible's opening chapters. Once we go back to creation, we realize God intends for us to enjoy all kinds of worldly pursuits. Our God didn't put Adam in the Garden just to preach and pray. The Lord has a far greater vision for us.

Sometimes it's hard to ponder the glory of life before the Fall. It's not easy to contemplate the Golden Age our first parents enjoyed, albeit briefly. It's hard to imagine what our lives would have been like if our ancestors had just ignored the serpent. All we've ever known is a broken, sinful and rebellious world.

I think that lots of believers struggle to understand how much we've lost. Life before the Fall seems so distant, so unreal. Reading names of trees like *Knowing Good and Evil* and *Life* doesn't click with modern readers. We're too far removed from ancient farming to appreciate what the Garden was like. But it was real—once.

Imagine for a moment waking up one morning refreshed, excited and full of joy. Beside you is your spouse, beautiful yet strong, consistent, always encouraging, always there for you. *Always.* The two of you share conversation that fills your deepest needs. Your spouse remains your very best friend—always understands and never lets you down. *Never.* You've never felt lonely, not even for a moment.

When you look back on your life, you have no regrets, no failures, no guilt. When people see your most secret inner life, there is nothing to be ashamed of. *Nothing.* You have no tensions in your life, no sorrows, no frustration, no loss. It just keeps getting better all the time.

You and your spouse spend time in prayer and worship, and you do so with no distractions, no little voice inside of you saying you're bored. Your worship energizes you. You always know and feel like God is right there with you. You don't struggle to pray.

God is near to you.

You get up and you're off to work. You always feel rested, full of energy and life. You love your job. It lines up exactly with your abilities, and you always feel like you're accomplishing a lot. It's a great act of worship, doing exactly what God wants you to do. You never dread work. *Never.*

You have everything you need and don't want anything else. There are no internal conflicts, mixed motives, critical words or complaints.

You have limitless youth but the experience and wisdom of age as well. And you still have your innocence. You're in perfect health and know you'll never die. God is with you.

You delight in everything you do, knowing your heart has a pure desire to glorify God. Think about that. A *pure and undivided desire* to honor, trust and obey the Lord. And everybody else shares that same heart.

You lost all of this in Genesis 3.

You lost the life God intended.

You lost the family life God intended, the job God intended, the prayer life God intended, the wholeness God intended.

We lost the society God intended.

Sometimes we forget what we had in that distant past. We fail to grieve the shattered relationships, the mixed motives, the anger and lust, the brokenness in ourselves and others, the violence that's engulfed creation. We come to accept the world in its current state. We're tempted to give up, shoving our political, educational and sexual lives into a separate drawer from our relationship with God.

The world is no longer the way God designed it. But the vision God gave Adam and Eve at creation remains God's vision for life upon the earth.

Go Back to the Old Testament

The first chapters of the Bible show us the world according to God. Even though sin has ravaged every area of our lives, God's creation still sets the norm—the ideal—for what life should be after the Fall. But going back to creation requires going back to the Old Testament, and a lot of Christians aren't really sure what to do with the Old Testament. Just look at the gilt edging on my Bible. The first three quarters are still shiny gold, with the exception of some worn spots in the Psalms. The New Testament, by contrast, is worn and white, the gold long since rubbed off.

Maybe you know that the first 75 percent of your Bible isn't worthless, but how do you know when something's "just an Old Testament thing" and when it applies to believers today? That's not a simple question, but at the very least we can say that the Old Testament does apply directly to our lives right now, especially if we have the added understanding given in the New Testament.

Remember the instruction Paul gave Timothy: "All Scripture is God-breathed and is useful for teaching, rebuking, correcting, and training in righteousness, so that the man of God may be thoroughly equipped for every good work" (2 Tim 3:16-17). It's easy to miss what Paul is telling us. The New Testament was only just being written down when the apostle penned these words.

While the New Testament is certainly Scripture, equal in status to the Old, Paul was speaking of the Law, the Prophets and the Writings—the Old Testament. One might even translate the passage, "The entire Old Testament is God-breathed." And we're supposed to use it! "The entire Old Testament is God-breathed *and is to be used* for teaching, rebuking, correcting and training in righteousness."

Think of all we miss if we jump right to the New Testament. The New Testament doesn't have a love song in it, for example. But God has given us a love song between a husband and wife—Song of Songs—to remind us that romance is a good part of his creation, not a secular vice! Without the first three quarters of the Bible, we could fall into an otherworldly spirituality that is not at all what God has given us. Our lives lose their wholeness when we contemplate salvation apart from creation. An authentic spirituality looks to all the Scripture.

Jesus upheld the authority of all of God's word. He told his disciples, "Do not think that I have come to abolish the Law or the Prophets; I have not come to abolish them but to fulfill them. I tell you the truth, until heaven and earth disappear, not the smallest letter, not the least stroke of a pen, will by any means disappear until everything is accomplished" (Mt 5:17-18).

Jesus looked back to creation when the Jewish teachers questioned him about divorce. God had permitted divorce within the state of Israel as a political necessity in Deuteronomy 24. But Jesus taught that, though legal, divorce had never been moral.

Why should the people have known divorce was immoral? Because they should have looked back to God's original design for marriage. Jesus explained, "Moses permitted you to divorce because your hearts were hard. *But it was not this way from the beginning.* I tell you that anyone who divorces his wife, except for marital unfaithfulness, and marries another woman commits adultery" (Mt 19:8-9, emphasis mine). God's original pattern for creation sets the standard. To know what God wants, we look back to creation.

Creation sets the pattern, a pattern greatly damaged by the Fall that broke our union with God. But even in the Old Testament, God begins the creation's redemption, giving laws to Israel to regulate every sphere of life. And Jesus came to accomplish creation's salvation, to restore that lost wholeness.

Ultimately, God's goal is not to have saved souls flittering about on clouds, but to rule over a restored creation. The creation itself is waiting for Jesus' return when it "will be liberated from its bondage to decay and brought into the glorious freedom of the children of God" (Rom 8:21). Our hope is of a wholeness to life in which all of God's creatures dance together to the praise and delight of our Father. I remember one seminary professor's remark: "The whole creation will be saved; it's only sinful humans who will be condemned."

Just look at the closing chapters of the Bible. They sound a lot like the first chapters of the Bible, don't they? Indeed, this heaven is not up in the sky. The New Jerusalem descends upon a renewed *earth* (Rev 21:2). Our heavenly future will be an earthly paradise.

Despite all the sin that has defiled this earth, God still isn't willing to scrap Plan A. He's going to return and fix the creation, burn up the sin and make everything the way it was intended to be when he designed it. What will the world be? What should the world be? Look back to creation. This is where our *whole* Christian worldview begins.

Go Back to God's Perspective

A worldview is just what it says: a view or perspective on the world. Worldviews are the glasses through which we see and understand (or misunderstand) the world around us. Everybody has a worldview. We all

have ways we look at life, an understanding—whether right or wrong—
of our universe. But a worldview is not merely an intellectual commitment. It shapes our souls, moves our affections, colors the way we interpret events and tells us how we should live.

When I was teaching theology at a college in Ukraine, I remember
asking my students, most of whom had grown up under communist
Soviet rule, "Did the communists have a perspective on education?" Yes.
On religion? Yes. Economics? Yes. Though doomed to fail from the start,
communism spread over half the globe because it provided a perspective
on all of reality. Communism provided a comprehensive life system
within which everything could make sense, a story about liberating the
masses from capitalism, a drama in which everyone played an important
part. Communism gave people meaning. The early communists were
willing to give up everything for their worldview. No sacrifice was too
great for the cause.

One of the biggest reasons the people of the former Soviet Union are
so discouraged today is because their worldview has failed them. The
way they looked at life—their vision of reality—is now gone, and they
aren't sure how to replace it. You can see the brokenheartedness on the
people's faces. They bet everything, and they lost their significance, their
purpose for living. The glue that held their society together has dried up
and fallen away. They no longer know how to make sense of their
world.

If we're going to live life as God intends it, we're first of all going to
have to see all of life as God himself sees it—*the world according to God.*
Our hearts will only find long-term satisfaction in a biblical worldview, a
God-centered perspective that is the only one that will last. The Christianity of the Bible is a comprehensive life system, a total way of seeing
and living in God's world, a perspective on life that begins with God the
Creator making everything out of nothing.

I'm old enough to remember the world before microwave ovens. Back
then when we wanted a fast meal, we gently slid an aluminum tray out of
a cardboard box, plopped it in the oven at 375° for forty-five minutes. The
aluminum TV dinner tray gives us a beautiful picture of the worldview.

Imagine the tray as your perspective on life. Within this worldview all the areas of your life are placed. The turkey and gravy might represent your job as an engineer or homemaker or social worker. Unless you have to wear a beeper, it stays in its compartment. In another compartment you find mashed potatoes—your family life. The green beans meanwhile stay to themselves. They represent entertainment. The most important part of your life is your relationship with God—that's the "cherry surprise" in the tray's middle compartment. I always loved the cherry surprise.

The problem with this image is that we're squeezing our relationship with God into a tiny compartment of our lives. Such religion can never satisfy; it will only fragment our lives. And besides, Jesus doesn't want to be cherry surprise. He wants to be the tray that holds every part of our lives. God doesn't want *to be in* our lives; he wants *to be* our lives. All of life is our relationship with God. Only when we find our wholeness in God himself will all the spheres of our lives hold together.

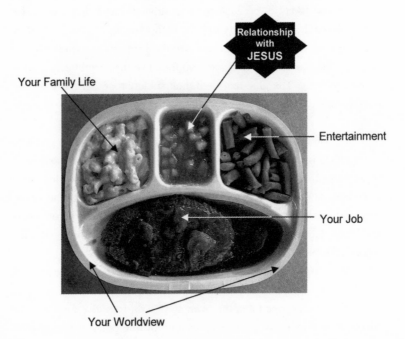

No area of your life will truly satisfy your heart until it becomes part of something larger than yourself. God didn't design you to be all about yourself but about him and his rule in the universe. I remember one friend coming to a humbling realization: "You know, the kingdom of God isn't all about *me.*" God doesn't exist for the other areas of our lives. The other areas of our lives exist for God.

God doesn't want you to fit your relationship with him into the TV tray the world gives you. Instead, God wants every area of your life—work and play, sexuality and civic engagement, art and music, education and sufferings, devotions and thinking, *everything*—to be part of a wonderful meal he's cooking.

God wants your life to look like this:

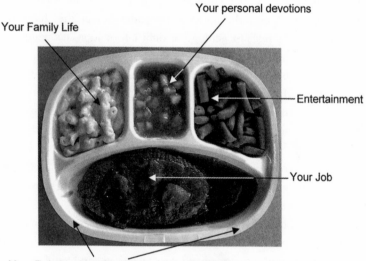

God wants your life to look like this:

Your personal devotions

Your Family Life

Entertainment

Your Job

Your Relationship with Jesus = Your Worldview

Doesn't that look better? I don't know. Maybe the illustration breaks down at this point because God hasn't promised us a wonderful TV dinner but a great feast. Still, the point remains valid. If you aren't developing a total Christian worldview, then you're subjecting your life to human patterns of living. Scripture instructs us: "Do not be conformed any longer to the pattern of this world, but be transformed by the renewing of your mind" (Rom 12:2).

The "pattern of this world" doesn't refer to any particular sin, or even to a lot of sins, but to the whole way of looking at life according to human perspectives. We are designed to see things and to live according to the pattern God gives us in creation and throughout the Bible. God promises that when we're getting our minds renewed by Scripture, then his truth transforms us inside and out.

Go Back to God's Categories

Educators have come to realize the powerful role mental categories play in learning. A child, for example, only comes to understand the difference between cats and dogs when realizing that cats and dogs are both in the animal category, but *cat* and *dog* are different categories within that big category. Cats and dogs aren't the same, though they have similarities. Learning is not just getting the right information. It's getting the right categories to interpret the information.

I used to have a ferret named Nancy Reagan. I remember when my cousin's little girl came over and saw Nancy. "Look at the kitty!" she cried. No, I explained. Nancy Reagan was not a kitty. Nancy Reagan was a ferret. Ferrets are smaller, skinnier and cause fewer allergies than kitties. But to her, there was only one category for all small, furry animals. As a result, the concept of the *ferret* found no place in her thinking. We learn by creating different mental compartments, different categories, which together form the grid for understanding our world.

Where do you get your categories? Does engineering fit into the *worldly callings of no eternal value* category? Or into the *jobs that pay big bucks* category? Or into the *good callings of God* category? Similarly, does sex fall under the *sin* category or the *gift of God* category—and are there other categories beneath these? Whose grid are you using?

What happens if we Christians conform our thinking to the pattern of this world? Can we just add Jesus to the world's TV tray? If the tray you've learned to think with is all about gaining personal peace and prosperity, for example, when you squeeze in Jesus, he will be crucified, not to make you righteous, but to lift your self-esteem. God gives you his commands, not to show you what delights him, but to show you how to get wealthy. Sin isn't bad because it offends a holy God but because it only leads to discouragement in the end.

Sound familiar? This is Christianity as cherry surprise. This is God as if God existed for us, not we for him. Placing Christianity within a non-Christian worldview is idolatry. The old maxim "everything in moderation" doesn't apply to Jesus Christ. God's word must structure our thinking about everything—not just "religious" topics; anything less is a compromised faith.

Further, if we aren't looking at the world from God's perspective, then we'll start looking at God from the world's perspective. It's just like Jesus warned us; "No one can serve two masters. Either he will hate the one and love the other, or he will be devoted to the one and despise the other" (Mt 6:24). Our souls long to know only one master: Jesus our Redeemer.

Go Back to Theology

Of course, understanding God's perspective on this world requires us to "do some theology," some serious thinking about God, the Bible, and this universe. We need to struggle with God's word and seek out what God is saying to the churches—and to us. Yet it seems that whenever I speak of our neediness for theology, some Christians have a knee-jerk reaction: "I don't need theology! I just love Jesus!"

I'm well aware that dead orthodoxy has always been a curse within the churches. I've seen it. I've been around people who do theology as an abstract science, usually with unbelief in their hearts—theologians who have no passion for God. Nothing angers me more than men and women who devote themselves to studying the Scripture without letting it touch their hearts. But the biblical alternative to dead orthodoxy is not ignorance but *living* orthodoxy.

Theology literally means "the study of God." Theology is the rigorous pursuit of God's truth as he explains it in the Scriptures. Does this sound too intellectual? Does this undercut a vibrant love of Jesus? I don't think so. If you really love Jesus, don't you want to know what he's said?

The conviction that theology isn't necessary because we already have Jesus is itself a powerful theological assertion. It's an affirmation that Jesus must be central to everything we do. It's a theological statement about how Jesus Christ satisfies our deepest human longings. To that extent, I can agree with it.

Actually, everyone is a theologian. Everyone has thoughts about God—even the atheist says in his heart, "There is no God," which is a statement about God and therefore theology. The question isn't whether or not you're a theologian. You already are. The real question is whether you're a good or bad theologian. To be a good theologian—regardless of your profession—you'll have to think hard about everything from God's perspective, the world according to God.

Remember the Lord's greatest commandment: to love God with all our minds as well as our hearts and souls (Mt 22:37). Our Father lays claim to our whole persons, our intellects included. Sure, God wants us to have a childlike faith, a trust in him that accepts whatever he says as the final word. But Scripture also tells us, "Brothers, stop thinking like children. In regard to evil be infants, but in your thinking be adults" (1 Cor 14:20). Paul warns us to "be very careful, then, how you live—not as unwise but as wise" (Eph 5:15).

Can theology answer every question we bring to it? No. The Christian theologian—the Christian who sets his heart and mind to the study of God—is always limited by God's self-revelation. We can only know what God has chosen to reveal about himself and his world. This limitation was stressed early in Israel's history. "The secret things belong to the LORD our God, but the things revealed belong to us and to our children forever, that we may follow in all the words of this law" (Deut 29:29).

It's been said that doing theology is like putting a puzzle together with half the pieces missing. God doesn't tell us everything—but he has told us all we need to know to be who he wants us to be. And he gives us enough anchors for our thought—enough categories—for us to make sense, though not perfect sense, of the world he has given us. As Christians go back to theology—applying Christian minds to the world we live in—we can increasingly delight in the wonder of God's creation and the wonder of creation's God. Our spiritual stomachs hunger for the solid food that discerns the difference between our Creator's good design and the corruptions we have added (Heb 5:14).

Your Soul Wants to Be More Than Saved

I'm convinced that every believer longs to integrate his or her faith in Christ with the rest of life. Christianity without theological reflection on all spheres of life has little power to transform ourselves, let alone our world. Living a Christian life without a Christian worldview is like trying to drive a truck without gasoline. So long as it's all downhill, you're okay. But as soon as the terrain gets nasty, you're out of fuel and find your life going nowhere.

I once heard a preacher tell a story about three stonemasons. In the Middle Ages building a cathedral was hard and tedious work. Masons would chisel block after block for their entire lives and maybe only complete a small section of wall. One day a man walked up to one of the masons and asked, "What are you doing?" He replied, "I'm wasting my time. I've worked all day and made no progress. I'm hot. I'm tired, and I want to go home." It was an honest answer. I know—I've been there!

So the man walked up to a second stonemason and asked, "What are you doing?" This one explained, "I'm finishing the upper edge on this stone. I've finished the lower edge and hope to have it ready for placement in a few weeks." This man evidently had some sense of the value of his work. Perhaps he even enjoyed his work.

And then our observer went to a third stonemason and asked, "What are you doing?" The stonemason, with a glimmer in his eye, pointed up to the towers high above and shouted, "I'm building a mighty cathedral to the glory of God!"

This stonemason understood that his little work was part of something far bigger than himself. We need to understand the big picture. We need to see how our day-to-day lives, even if they're tedious and hard and don't seem at all religious, fit into God's purpose for planet earth. Then we can find the joy and strength to do all we do to the glory of God.

God designed us to live in a complex web of relationships with people and institutions, ourselves and nature, in which all our relationships are but different opportunities to rejoice in his goodness, power and life with single-minded devotion.

Certainly all of these relationships have been damaged and continue to be damaged by our corporate and individual rebellion against him. But there is hope even for the messiest area of your life, whether family, work, sex or whatever. God offered his Son in your place. As one child put it, "God spanked Jesus instead of me." Our God has obligated himself to receive any sinner who comes to him grieving his rebellion and looking to Jesus for help. God forgives, and he does a lot more.

Jesus came to do more than forgive you; he came to establish a kingdom—God's rule upon the earth (Mt 4:17). Even in the Great Commission, Jesus' final marching orders for the church, Jesus calls us to do more than preach forgiveness, a lot more than "getting saved." Jesus instructs us to teach all the nations to obey everything the Lord commands (Mt 28:20). This certainly starts with forgiveness. But if we're to grow to be what God wants us to be, we'll need more. To live all of life as God intends it means we need to see life as God sees it. If we're going to be more than saved, we're going to have to ponder the world according to God, to understand what God intends the brass to look like.

Starting in the first three chapters of Genesis, we'll look at different areas of life first introduced in the book of beginnings: people, authority, human culture, work, science and education, sex and sexuality, communication, the human condition, God's relationship with us, and finally suffering, death and the life beyond it. Beginning in the beginning we can develop a total Christian worldview. All of these different areas of life have their source in God's creative energy.

In a world that seems so fragmented and compartmentalized, where we suffer from information overload, we long for wholeness. If we look at the different spheres of our lives and see a dozen unrelated branches shooting off in different directions, it's helpful to step back and see where all the branches came from, to follow them down to the trunk from which each branch springs. Here we can follow the advice of the Dutch theologian and prime minister Abraham Kuyper, who in 1898 delivered these words to the faculty of Princeton:

> *Such a life system [must] find its starting point in a special interpretation of*
> *our relation to God. . . . If such an action is to put its stamp upon our entire*
> *life, it must start from that point in our consciousness in which our life is*
> *still undivided and lies comprehended in its unity,—not in the spreading*
> *vines but in the root from which all the vines spring. . . . Here alone we find*
> *the common source from which the different streams of our human life*
> *spring and separate themselves.*[1]

So this is where our worldview begins—where our universe begins, where our lives begin and where the Bible begins: "In the beginning, God."

Questions for Discussion

1. How would you respond to the question, Why polish the brass if the ship is sinking?

2. Why do you think many Christians spend less time in the Old Testament than in the New? What might we miss by focusing only on the New Testament?

3. Many believers seem satisfied with life in this world. What do you make of that? Of what other problems may it be a symptom?

4. How might you answer if a Christian architecture student asked you, "What does designing buildings have to do with the kingdom of God?" How does your current occupation fit into God's bigger scheme?

5. What do you see as creation's past, present and future? How does this perspective influence the way you live your life today?

6. Do you ever long for wholeness in your life? If God doesn't want to *be in* your life so much as *being* your life, how can you know the difference?

7. Of the different areas these chapters will examine *(God, people, authority, culture, work, science and education, sex and sexuality, communication, the human condition, God's relationship with us, and suffering, death and the afterlife)*, in which one do you most long to see God at work in your life?

---

[1] Abraham Kuyper, *Lectures on Calvinism* (Grand Rapids, Mich.: Eerdmans, 1931), p. 20.

2

HAS GOD MELLOWED WITH AGE?

God According to God

"In the beginning, God . . ."
GENESIS 1:1

Our souls long for unity. We hunger to see the many spheres of life as branches spreading from the great trunk, which is God. This is what we need. But this unity means nothing if we start with the wrong trunk.

Getting the Right God: Exodus 32:1-10
It's so easy for us fallen sinners to start with the wrong God. The best heresies have always originated with wrong assumptions about God. The Mormons say that God used to be a man like us, created by a different god at some earlier date. Little Yahweh grew up on a world like our own and lived a righteous Mormon lifestyle, through which he earned godhood and his own universe to rule. Centuries earlier Muhammad insisted that God must be so transcendent—so otherworldly—that he could never unite himself to a human nature—and from this assumption he rejected Jesus both as God in the flesh and as Savior of the world.

Nothing matters more than what you think about God. A phony deity can never answer the questions of human life. Still, human history—including the history of God's people—is filled with attempts to change the face of almighty God.

When we Christians read the Old Testament, we often think *we're better than those dumb Israelites*. But the Old Testament story is our story, too, and it is our God—not some other God—who dealt with our spiritual ancestors at Sinai. When we read the Old Testament, we don't identify with God's appointed mediator Moses or with God, but with those sinful Israelites.

So what did we do while Moses talked with God?

> *Now when the people saw that Moses delayed to come down from the mountain, the people assembled about Aaron, and said to him, "Come, make us a god who will go before us; as for this Moses, the man who brought us up from the land of Egypt, we do not know what has become of him." And Aaron said to them, "Tear off the gold rings which are in the ears of your wives, your sons, and your daughters, and bring them to me."*
>
> *Then all the people tore off the gold rings which were in their ears, and brought them to Aaron. And he . . . made it into a molten calf; and they said, "This is your god, O Israel, who brought you up from the land of Egypt."*
>
> *Now when Aaron saw this, he built an altar before it; and Aaron made a proclamation and said, "Tomorrow shall be a feast to the LORD." So the next day they rose early and offered burnt offerings, and brought peace offerings; and the people sat down to eat, and rose up to play. (Ex 32:1-6 NASB)*

According to the Israelites they weren't turning away from God when they worshiped the golden calf. They refer to the golden calf as their god, specifically, the one that brought them out of Egypt. They said this was their God, literally *Elohim*. Later they refer to it as the LORD—*Yahweh* in the original Hebrew.

They had no intention of changing deities. They were just making God a little more reliable, a little more visible. Sure, God doesn't look anything like the image they created, but he doesn't look like the old man or the shiny light that many of us visualize when we pray.

What was really happening according to God?

Then the LORD spoke to Moses, "Go down at once, for your people, whom you brought up from the land of Egypt, have corrupted themselves. They have quickly turned aside from the way which I commanded them. They have made for themselves a molten calf, and have worshiped it, and have sacrificed to it, and said, 'This is your god, O Israel, who brought you up from the land of Egypt!'" And the LORD said to Moses, "I have seen this people, and behold, they are an obstinate people. Now then let me alone, that my anger may burn against them, and that I may destroy them; and I will make of you a great nation." (Ex 32:7-10 NASB)

From their own perspective the Israelites at Sinai were worshiping Yahweh their God. They just pictured Yahweh a little differently. Cows are good things. And why wouldn't God be happy to be pictured in gold? Their mistake—and ours—was to think that they could redefine God so as to better fill their needs.

God saw things differently than our spiritual forefathers. If the Israelites saw a little theological redefinition, God saw a turning away, an apostasy, the worship of another God. The calf was not God. If you have the wrong God, nothing else matters. You can pray until you're blue in the face and sing praise choruses until you're hoarse. It's all worthless. You have the wrong God.

Exodus 32 warns believers to watch what we think about God. Perhaps a new and improved Yahweh will smooth out your philosophy, improve your apologetic with unbelievers or make your God more rational or more human. But from God's perspective, it's idolatry. This question is the most important question you'll ever consider. Who is God—the real God—according to God?

What God Is Like
The very first words of Genesis, "In the beginning God," speak to the fact that the God who later entered into covenant with Abraham—the God and Father of our Lord Jesus Christ—is not dependent on anything outside of himself. He is self-existent. When God brought the universe into being, at this earliest moment in history God had already existed forever.

God has always existed in all his perfection. When there was nothing else, God reigned over that nothingness with eternal power and excellence. Any attempt to contemplate him has to begin with a humble recognition of God's infinity, his incomprehensibility. God doesn't need us, as Paul told the philosophers in Athens:

> *The God who made the world and everything in it is Lord of heaven and earth and does not live in temples built by hands. And he is not served by human hands, as if he needed anything, because he himself gives all men life and breath and everything else. From one man he made every nation of men, that they should inhabit the whole earth; and he determined the times set for them and the exact places where they should live. (Acts 17:24-25)*

God is completely self-sufficient, while we are dependent upon him for our very existence. God determined that you would live, and when and where you would live. But nothing has ever determined God.

Being First, Doing Second

If I've seen it once, I've seen it a thousand times. Christians are asked in a worship service or prayer meeting to offer praise to God. And then they thank God for saving them, for sending Jesus, for having mercy upon them. Thanksgiving is good, but there is a difference between praising and thanking. We praise people for *who they are*. We thank people for *what they've done*.

Imagine a friend of mine telling me about his fiancée for the first time. He says, "Greg, I'd like you to meet my fiancée. She helps me with my calculus homework." *Okay,* I think. So I ask him to tell me about her, and he responds, "She helped me pass that nasty midterm last week." That's wonderful, but what's so awesome about this woman? "She showed me how to integrate equations. Without her I'd have been toast."

What's wrong with this picture?

I'm not asking what she's done to help you. What she's like? Yet Americans are trained to put doing before being. When we meet people, often we first ask what they do for a living. Isn't their character, their personal qualities more important? Any relationship that centers only on what someone has to offer is a relationship destined to fail.

Millions of Christians claim to have a personal relationship with God, but when I hear them pray, I wonder how personal that relationship really is. Does it center on God's person or only on his benefits?

Biblically speaking we know God both through his actions—his mighty deeds—and through propositions about him in Scripture, statements that describe who he is and what he's like. Much of theology in the twentieth century looked to God's actions alone, specifically to human experiences of God, rather than to what he explicitly says about himself in the Bible. I think this was a huge mistake, and the further theologians went with this mistake, the less Christian their theologies became.

The knowledge of God begins with this truth implanted within our humanity. Before Jesus—God incarnate—revealed the Father to humanity, before the prophets spoke to Israel by the Holy Spirit, or before he called Abram to leave the land of his fathers and enter into covenant with God—before all of this—God had already communicated clearly who he was.

Paul explains in the beginning of Romans how God's power, eternity and divine nature have been known by all people since creation (Rom 1:20). This knowledge is native to our humanity—though it's a knowledge of God that people suppress because of their sin (Rom 1:23). The created world itself demonstrates not only who God is but also something of his character—his moral law, his loves and hates (Rom 1:32).

But sin has so affected our willingness to hear creation's message that when God entered history to save a people for himself, he gave them further communication. This revelation has been passed down to us in the form of our Bible. From Scripture we see far more clearly who God is. We see not only God as Creator but also God as Redeemer. But realize that the biblical documents do not just give us God according to human reflection. This is God according to God.

Knowing God According to God
We've already spoken of God's self-existence and self-sufficiency. There's a lot God shows us about himself. He tells us he's a spirit, not a material being. The God who created the visible universe is himself invisible (Col

1:15; 1 Tim 1:17); therefore, he instructs us not to visualize him or make pictures of him (Deut 4:15-18).

But God is an omnipresent spirit, not limited by space. He is everywhere, we say—though I think it's safer to say that *everywhere* is always in God's presence, since God is bigger than everywhere. Paul told the Athenians, "He is not far from each one of us. For in him we live and move and have our being" (Acts 17:27-28).

Indeed, we can say God has no limitations at all outside of himself, a fact Isaiah drives home (Is 40:12-26). God is not limited by time but has always existed, "from everlasting to everlasting" (Is 40:28; Ps 90:2). Nor is God limited in his knowledge. He knows all, even the thoughts of people's hearts. Thus, we say he is omniscient (Rom 11:33-36).

But the limitless God who entered history tells us further that he is a holy God. Holiness involves both moral purity and otherness. God has no darkness within him, and he is thoroughly unlike everything else. Winged cherubim cry day and night, "Holy, holy, holy is the LORD Almighty" (Is 6:3). It's the background noise of heaven, eternally repeated for infinite emphasis. He is "majestic in holiness, awesome in glory, working wonders" (Ex 15:11).

God's holiness means he is just as well as loving. He always pays back sin appropriately (2 Thess 1:5-10). And his wrath is not just an "Old Testament thing"—most biblical references to hell are in the New Testament. God hasn't mellowed with age. He is a wrathful God (Jn 3:36) who jealously guards his own glory (Is 48:11). Even the believer's sins are punished—Jesus takes that punishment in our place.

The cross thus displays God's justice and love for all to see. "God is love" (1 Jn 4:8). Indeed, God's character is the very standard for what is and is not loving. God is merciful to those who suffer, Jesus displaying for us God's compassion on the crowds (Mt 9:36). Our God is generous, feeding the birds and us (Mt 6:26).

God can be relied on. He is truthful in all he says and does. Paul says we can believe God's promises because "God . . . does not lie" (Tit 1:2). And God is faithful. He never breaks a promise. "He is the faithful God, keeping his covenant of love to a thousand generations of those who love him and keep his commandments" (Deut 7:9). I know of people who have left their spouses saying, "I'm no longer the person I was when I married you." God will never pull a trick like that. God "does not change like the shifting shadows" (Jas 1:17).

Some biblical passages say that God sometimes "changes his mind" or "repents" (Gen 6:5-6; 1 Sam 15:11). Still, God tells us explicitly, "I the LORD do not change" (Mal 3:6). God promised judgment on Nineveh, but when the citizens repented, God withheld that judgment (Jon 3:10). The real change in these instances is not in *who God is* but in the *people* God addresses. God deals with the humble differently than the proud, but he doesn't change who he is or what he's like.

I've heard a few theologians warn about the danger of describing God with lists of characteristics or attributes. They fear it risks depersonalizing God, making him into a series of propositions rather than a Person. I understand their concern. But to describe your wife as patient does not depersonalize her into the abstraction of patience. We can describe God with statements—propositions—just like he describes himself. But the warning is a valid one. It's possible to know *about* God without actually knowing God.

Our God is a God who acts. Still, God's actions aren't self-interpreting. (How many times have you tried to figure out what someone's actions meant?) Rather, our God tells us what his actions mean. We only understand God's actions because we understand *who it is* who is acting, *what he's like*, and *what passions* motivate his actions. The great deeds our God has done in history remind us what God explicitly tells us about himself:

> *The LORD, the LORD, the compassionate and gracious God, slow to anger, abounding in love and faithfulness, maintaining love to thousands, and forgiving wickedness, rebellion and sin. Yet he does not leave the guilty unpunished; he punishes the children and their children for the sin of the fathers to the third and fourth generation. (Ex 34:6-7)*

Idolo Lluvia Meets the Kids

I'm about to let you in on a dark, dirty secret: I actually have two gods—one that I worship and another one that I just pull out of a bag when I need him to prove a point. A second god can be helpful when you need to illustrate something. This extra deity came in handy some time ago while I was teaching a class of ten- and eleven-year-old kids about God.

I was telling them how great my god is. "He is there whenever I need him. Wherever I go, my god can go with me. In fact, he's with me today, right here in this room." All the while the kids were nodding in agreement.

Then I casually pulled my *idolo lluvia*—my Mayan rain god—out of a paper sack. At eighteen inches tall this little guy is the best terra cotta deity Pier One sells. I took him by the head and plopped him down in the center of the table.

I wondered, *Are these kids too young to understand the attributes of God?* I imagined nasty phone calls from angry parents. Was I going to have to face a heresy trial for promoting native idols? Nevertheless, in the face of serious doubts, I plunked *idolo lluvia* down on the table. In the distance I could hear the proverbial pin drop. Loudly. But the response didn't take too long.

One ten-year-old girl jumped up and shouted, "That's not God!"

"How do you know?" I demanded.

"Because the Bible says that God is a *spirit.* That means he's *invisible.* And I can see *that!*"

Another kid pointed out that the real God is eternal, and my *idolo lluvia* has "Made in Mexico" stamped right on his backside. And then God is unchanging; *idolo lluvia* was missing an ear from the time I accidentally kicked him over. These children also explained that the god on the table was not omnipotent, omniscient or omnipresent but was limited in every way. And he was definitely not holy. He looks sort of like a planter, actually.

Sure, God's not a list of attributes. But he has told us what he's like; therefore, we need to listen. Can we ever fully comprehend God? Of course not. But we can apprehend what he's communicated about himself. So as we contemplate God in all his perfections, I'd like to point out one false god that I think particularly demands Christians' allegiance today. Though more sophisticated than *idolo lluvia*, he's just as false as the golden calf the Israelites called the LORD.

The Deist God Versus the Sovereign God

The deist heresy, which flourished in eighteenth-century England, was a movement within the churches that sought to rid God of his sovereignty. *Sovereignty* refers to God's kingship over history, his direction of all things toward his desired outcome. A sovereign God is in control. The deists, by contrast, proposed a "clockwork" deity. God created the universe, then exited stage left, taking a nap while human history progressed. Instead of God working out his eternal purposes in history, natural laws and chance ruled history.

I wish I could say that deism was eradicated in the eighteenth century.

But I suspect that deism is the most prevalent heresy within Christendom today. When I talk about the wrath of God or hell, a few people in the pews fidget. But when I say God controls everything, most of them fidget and a few drop their jaws in horror. Deism has become the religion of the American people. Deism guarantees that our actions are free from God's intervention. But God sees himself as one who is in control.

Certainly God knows what's going to happen tomorrow. Knowledge of the future is a necessary attribute of deity in the Bible (Is 41:22-23; 42:8-9). This is why God established predictive prophecy as a test of true and false prophets (Deut 18:21-22). Jesus' ability to predict the future evidenced that he is *I am*, the God Moses encountered (Jn 13:21).

But Scripture presents more than God's foreknowledge. God establishes history. Nothing happens in this universe apart from his permission. Yes, human beings are free moral agents, responsible for their actions—that's why God can give us commands. Human beings make choices freely without coercion from God. And we know that God is not the author of evil. He doesn't tempt anyone to sin—the tendency toward evil flows from our character, not God's (Jas 1:13).

So does Scripture teach that we make our own choices, or that God controls everything?

Both are true. From a human perspective we witness chains of cause and effect. Storm clouds cause rain. But this can be called a *secondary cause*. A greater cause lies invisibly behind. If God were not holding all things together, there wouldn't be any clouds to cause the storm. Or any earth to receive the rain. God didn't just create the world like a watch and wind it up. The world can't keep ticking on its own. The world is less like a watch and more like a song.

To keep a song going requires continued action—it's not self-sustaining. God tells us that nature is sustained moment-by-moment by his own sovereign will. Christ himself is the glue in which "all things hold together" (Col 1:17). He is "sustaining all things by his powerful word" (Heb 1:3). The universe is not a static machine but a dynamic reality. If we look only at the secondary causes—like clouds that cause rain—then we fail to recognize the rain as a gift from the Father, the *First Cause* behind everything.

God is the invisible actor in the drama of history. He's also the author, even down to its details. It's *his*tory, after all. Because God wrote the whole play every sphere of life has significance. If God is in control of your health or your family or your finances or that biochemistry midterm tomorrow, then the monkey is off your back.

Every situation comes, at its most basic level, from the hand of the God who loves you. All of life, therefore, is a relationship with God, a response to the one in control when everything seems out of control. Questions about human freedom and responsibility aside, God's will is the supreme controlling influence behind everything that happens. So how far does God's control extend?

God controls nature. God is the first cause behind the secondary causes of nature:

> *He makes clouds rise from the ends of the earth;*
> *he sends lightning with the rain*
> *and brings out the wind from his storehouse. (Ps 135:7)*

While we work and farm and shop for food, it's really God's hand that feeds us, just as he feeds the birds (Mt 6:26-30). The lions seek their food from God (Ps 104:21), just as Elijah was fed by ravens directed by God (1 Kings 17:4-6).

God gives us our circumstances. Daniel praised God not only for overruling nature but also empires: "He changes times and seasons, / he sets up kings and deposes them" (Dan 2:20-21). Paul reminds us that the civil authorities rule by God's choosing and are to be honored (Rom 13:1), even though those rulers were living in rebellion against God.

On a more personal level, the circumstances of our individual lives are ordered by God's decree. Hear how Hannah's great prayer rebukes the myth of the self-made man: "The LORD brings death and makes alive; / he brings down to the grave and raises up. / The LORD sends poverty and wealth; / he humbles and he exalts" (1 Sam 2:6-7). And since God is the one who numbers the hairs of my head (Mt 10:30)—and that number is already shrinking—I can trust my future into my Father's loving care.

God overrules free choices. Even free *human* choices, while not coerced, are nevertheless made within and under the sovereign plan of God. When the Egyptians favored the Israelites, it was because God had said, "I will make the Egyptians favorably disposed toward this people" (Ex 3:21; 12:36). Conversely, when Pharaoh hardened his heart against God, it was because God was hardening Pharaoh's heart (Ex 10:20). Even the most heinous crime in human history—the murder of God in the flesh—while committed by responsible (and guilty) free agents, was nevertheless "by God's set purpose and foreknowledge" (Acts 2:23). The disciples affirmed, "They did what your power and will had decided beforehand should happen" (Acts 4:28).

God directs the angels and—yes—even the devil himself. God tells us both that he incited David to take a census of the people (2 Sam 24:1) and that Satan incited David to take the census (1 Chron 21:1). Is this a contradiction? No. Satan only does what God permits. Satan could only torment Job with God's permission—and even then God placed limits upon him, forbidding him to kill Job (Job 1:12). Our sovereign king oversees everything. The angels "do his bidding" (Ps 103:20-21).

God orders everything. Romans 8:28 reminds us that God has a purpose even when we can't see it. And God's purpose for his people is to make us like Jesus. "And we know that in all things, God works for the good of those who love him, who have been called according to his purpose" (Rom 8:28). "All things" means nothing escapes God's eternal purpose in Christ. "In him we were also chosen, having been predestined according to the plan of him who works out everything in conformity with the purpose of his will" (Eph 1:11).

And the context in Ephesians 1 is immense. Paul is speaking of God's purpose to bring "all things in heaven and on earth" together under the rule of Jesus Christ (1:9-10). Everything here means everything. Accidents are not accidental. Both good times and bad come from the hand of the same God.

> Who can speak and have it happen
>   if the Lord has not decreed it?
> Is it not from the mouth of the Most High
>   that both calamities and good things come? (Lam 3:37-38)

The God of many church people today is not a sovereign God. He is a powerless bystander. The God that many have invented in their hearts does not give calamities, and even good things are as likely to be considered coincidences. But this is not *your* God, O Christian! Such a man-made God does not have supreme power—who could fear such a God? The only antidote to deism is to see God according to God. The Lord is totally sovereign, directing even the tiniest details in absolute accord with his eternal plan for history.

But in God's mystery, we aren't puppets. When I teach the sovereignty of God I'm always asked, "Does this mean we're puppets?" No. We don't have to choose either a sovereign God or responsible people. Both are truth. Puppets don't have wills or make choices. They have no desires, thoughts, loves or hates. People do. But the mystery of God's power is that while we mortals make our plans, God establishes his own plans. And God is powerful enough to see his plan accomplished by our plans—even when we are unwilling to cooperate. God works invisibly behind the scenes so that his plan always includes and often overrules ours. God's good plan always trumps our evil plans.

This was certainly the case in Joseph's life. Joseph's brothers burned with jealousy against him and they sold him into slavery. The brothers had their plans, which were evil. But God had his own plan, a good one. While the brothers sent Joseph into Egypt, so did God. With the eyes of faith Joseph tells his brothers, "So then, it was not you who sent me here, but God" (Gen 45:8). God's plan trumped theirs.

Joseph himself later explained to his brothers, "You intended to harm me, but God intended it for good to accomplish what is now being done, the saving of many lives" (Gen 50:20). Were they all puppets? No. But they weren't totally sovereign, either. Their free choices took place under the control of a God with his own agenda.

God's total sovereignty isn't a theological abstraction. The real beauty of God's sovereignty comes in knowing that he controls circumstances that seem out of control to us. This is why we can trust God. Why ask his help if he couldn't do anything? Why pray for a friend's salvation if God has no power over the sinner's heart? But we are called to pray continuously (1 Thess 5:17), and God assures us that he can change the world when we ask him (2 Cor 1:11; Jas 5:15).

Of course, this has practical implications during hard times. You can know that whatever comes your way, it comes under the sovereign plan of a God who loves you. Don't ever tell someone who's suffering that God has nothing to do with his or her suffering. The last thing I want to be told when I'm suffering is that my pain has no eternPal significance. When we look from God's perspective, we realize that God orders every disappointment, loss and sorrow as surely as he brings us every joy.

This was Job's faith when he lost everything. "The LORD gave and the LORD has taken away; / may the name of the LORD be praised" (Job 1:21). God has a purpose we can't always see. Our sufferings and even our sin have significance. They are the rough stitches in the beautiful tapestry of God's plan. We see only rough stitches now, but at the end of the age, when we can take in the whole picture, we'll see that even the ugly stitches played a necessary part in the beautiful design.

Our God is in charge. We needn't fear that his plans will be thwarted.

Chance is an illusion. We're at no one's mercy but his. Let us remember Henry Blamires's sober warning:

> *If we try to change the face of eternal God, we indulge in the supreme idolatry, beside which perhaps, in the scale of sin, adultery weighs like a feather and murder like a farthing. Yet the sin is committed among us, within Christendom, within the Church—maybe within ourselves; for are we sure, after all, that we prayed to the true God this morning?*[1]

To see God according to God is to be passionately in love, not with a small God of our own making, but with the real God who is supreme. Scripture begins not with us but with God, eternally self-sufficient, needing nothing, but choosing to bring us into existence for his own purposes. Therefore, God must be supreme in our thoughts; his honor, his truth, his righteousness, love and mercy must dictate all else.

The real import of knowing a sovereign God, then, presses itself upon everything else in the coming chapters. When we look at God's world from his perspective, we're learning to live all of life under the rule of a God completely worthy of our trust, love, worship and obedience.

He sovereignly directs our paths so that our every choice becomes part of our relationship with him. Every job opportunity we take or leave, every difficult relationship we faithfully bear with, and every vote we cast is a direct response to the circumstances that God has sovereignly given us. We respond to the situations God puts us in either by faith or in unbelief. We either build his kingdom in every sphere of life or we rebel against him. Nothing is neutral.

I am convinced that the secret to overcoming a mediocre walk with God lies not in us but in the sovereign work of God. He must revive us. We ought to pray as Isaiah prayed while God's people were being chastened for their sins:

> *Look down from heaven and see*
> *from your lofty throne, holy and glorious.*

---

[1] Harry Blamires, *A God Who Acts: Recognizing the Hand of God in Suffering and Failure* (Ann Arbor, Mich.: Servant, 1981), p. 51.

Where are your zeal and your might?
  Your tenderness and compassion are withheld from us. . . .

You, O LORD, are our Father,
  our Redeemer from of old is your name.
Why, O LORD, do you make us wander from your ways
  and harden our hearts so we do not revere you?
Return for the sake of your servants,
  the tribes that are your inheritance. (Is 63:15-17)

Our zeal is dependent on God's zeal. He must return to us if we are to return to him. He is our Father. He is our Redeemer. We are his people, his treasured inheritance. Like God breathed upon the dry bones, awakening them into a vast army (Ezek 37:1-14), so in our day God must sovereignly breathe life into us to wake us to our own sin and even more so to his greatness. He lacks no power. Nothing takes him by surprise. The deists were wrong. Yahweh is not a mere spectator.

When we are awakened to God's greatness, our hearts become filled with a certainty of his coming triumph and a zeal that some call fanaticism. But Scripture instructs, "Never be lacking in zeal, but keep your spiritual fervor, serving the Lord" (Rom 12:11). Moment by moment our God gives us both our circumstances and the spiritual life to respond in faith. There are no accidents, only God-given opportunities to change the world in the power of the Holy Spirit.

When God awakens in us a passion for his majesty, we can make the most of every opportunity. But enjoying life as he designed it requires the humility to find our satisfaction in his perfections—not in our own (or lack thereof). As we meditate upon the character and attributes of our awesome God, this knowledge of God brings an ever-clearer knowledge of ourselves. To this knowledge of our humanity we now turn.

Questions for Discussion

1. List three things you realized more fully about God while reading this chapter.

2. How would you answer a believer who says, "It doesn't matter

what you believe about God so long as you love him"?

3. What's the difference between thanking God and praising God? How many characteristics of God can you think of that deserve your praise? Go through the alphabet—almighty, beautiful, the Creator and so on. Look at Psalms 89—101 for suggestions.

4. Meditate for a few minutes on each of the attributes (characteristics) of God mentioned in this chapter. What difference does each of God's qualities make in your life? How is each like humanity and how is each different? What is the opposite of each attribute?

5. What does it mean to say that God is sovereign? Putting any philosophical objections aside, what difference should God's sovereignty make in your life?

3

A HIGH, LOW OR
ACCURATE SELF-IMAGE?

People According to God

"So God created man in his own image."
GENESIS 1:27

For centuries people have considered what it means to be human. Plato defined the human being as a "featherless biped." While accurate, Plato's definition seems lacking. There's more to being human than having no feathers and walking on two feet. How does God see us, his human creatures?

Bent Inward on Ourselves

People in the postindustrial West have been more concerned with their own significance in recent decades than perhaps ever before. Maybe we suffer from our own material prosperity. We aren't worrying about whether we'll have food today. We have more time to ponder ourselves than our grandparents' generation ever had. Introspection and the depression it often breeds are common problems today. We've become a people bent inward on ourselves.

Every day I see people obsessed with how they feel about themselves. It's good that they realize the sickness of their soul. But when I look at Americans, I see a people too self-absorbed. Some of us see the brokenness within our souls and wallow in it.

Others among us are just as self-absorbed but tend to anesthetize themselves. They dull the pain of existence through pleasure. Rather than meditating on the brokenness of life, they get drunk or high or party or download a sex partner off the Internet. Others, however, choose a cleaner-looking anesthesia. They keep themselves too busy to ever have time to sit still and think. Just look at how we spend our time—always doing, never just being.

Even something that's supposed to relax us, like television, keeps us busy. The commercials throw a different image at you every second. Rush. Rush. Rush. And we put one of these glass and plastic stress boxes in every room of the house!

Furthermore, Americans are grossly overscheduled. When high school students need PalmPilots to keep track of their activities, something is wrong. We're busy, self-absorbed and lonely. We lack the ability to get beyond our own circumstances.

We need a vantage point from which to get the big picture. We need to know God's perspective, the only one that really matters. So we'll consider ourselves as God's creatures, as his image-bearers, as sinners and as saints. People aren't one-liners. The human soul has many facets. We begin with people as creatures.

A Humble Starting Point: The Human as Creature

Having begun this meditation on God's world with the infinite God himself, I'm struck by how puny I am beside one who holds the galaxies in his hand. He is eternal (1 Tim 1:17); I am mortal (Gen 6:3). His understanding is infinite (Ps 147:5); mine finite (Job 38:1—39:30). God is self-sufficient (Acts 17:24-25); I am derived and dependent forever upon him (Heb 1:3). He has life in himself (Jn 5:26); I have life on loan (Acts 17:25). First and foremost, I am but a creature.

So why did God create us? It's not because God *needed* to create us. When we start processing the actions of a sovereign and self-sufficient God through a need psychology, we've crossed the line into something other than Christianity. God has no needs, no felt needs and no love deficits. *We were not created because the Almighty was lonely.*

So why did God make us? We were created as good creatures—even "very good" by God's designation (Gen 1:31). God made us for a purpose beyond ourselves. We aren't what this universe is all about. We're God's *image*, not God himself. Like everything else in God's world, we're but means to a greater end. Our purpose lies not in ourselves but in the display of God's glory.

Remember the very first lie about God—the one the serpent told Eve. We'll spend more time in Eden in later chapters, but for now notice the nature of the serpent's deception. He told our first parents that they could be like God (Gen 3:5). This was the big one. Believing this lie got the first family expelled from Eden. This lie, which ruined it for us all, is a lie about us, about our place in the universe. But before that, it's a lie about God and his supremacy.

What exactly makes the serpent's lie so awful? God is good, what's the problem with trying to be like God?

The problem, of course, is that God is jealous, adamantly unwilling to share his glory with another. He really is God. We aren't. And deity has certain prerogatives. The serpent implied that it was wrong for God not to share. Kindergartners know you're supposed to share. *God shouldn't be so self-centered.* This was the first heresy, from which all other heresies flow.

Still, according to human standards it makes sense. God is good after all, and selfishness (for humans) is a bad thing. So God should treat us as equals. It sounds so liberating, so democratic, so very American. To say that God is rightly selfish rubs American Christians the wrong way. We've bought into the serpent's ethics. And like all heresy, such deception ultimately robs us of our humanness.

God Goes on Trial
But before going further, let's clear the air. Let's imagine the Almighty on trial for his crime.

THE TRIAL

DEFENDANT:	God
OCCUPATION:	Maker, ruler, judge of heavens and earth
ADDRESS:	Everywhere, particularly the heavens
CHARGE:	Being selfish

The prosecutors pile up reams of evidence. The most serious comes from the Defendant's own book. They cite

1. *Hell, Fires of. Billions will suffer there, and the Defendant says he will do it to "display his wrath" (Rom 9:22).*

2. *Intolerance of non-Christian religions. He calls them idolatry and says he will punish them (1 Cor 6:9-10).*

3. *Intolerance of numerous behaviors that people enjoy (Ex 20).*

4. *Insistence that people focus all attention on Defendant all the time. Intolerance toward those who do otherwise (1 Cor 10:31).*

The prosecutor points to the Defendant's burning to death two young men, Nadab and Abihu, for offering sacrifices in his own temple the Defendant hadn't commanded (Lev 10:1-7). Further, the Defendant struck dead a man named Uzzah for touching the Defendant's Ark of the Covenant in a sincere attempt to keep it from falling off its cart (2 Sam 6:6-8). On one occasion the Defendant killed everyone on earth but eight people (Gen 6-8).

More recently he took the lives of a married couple, Ananias and Sapphira, in order to make the church fear him, just because they'd lied to him when, in fact, they were giving money to the Defendant's own church (Acts 5:1-11). The Defendant thinks himself more important than other people. He thinks his rules are the only rules. The Defendant is selfish.

The Defendant steps up to the bench: "Guilty as charged."

Many passages in the Bible honestly trouble a lot of Christians—passages where God kills people, punishes people, seems intolerant, offensive, even selfish. Whenever a passage in the Bible rubs us the wrong way, it should give us pause because the problem is not with the Bible but with us.

What is it we don't understand about God's character that makes some of his actions seem so unfair? One simple truth—once grasped— unlocks a renewed understanding both of God and people. One single passion drives God's interactions with us: *God's primary concern in everything he does is to bring glory to himself.*

What? Who does God think he is? The center of the universe?

Yes. God is concerned with his own fame. Self-centered. Granted, as one rightly self-centered, he's been terribly generous, even giving his Son for our salvation (Jn 3:16). But God is supremely concerned with the honor of his name—just look at the prayer Jesus taught us to pray. Before ever getting to our needs, we pray for God's name to be honored and his kingdom to be furthered (Mt 6:9-13). This should put us in our place. We are just creatures, whose purpose lies outside ourselves.

With God, self-centeredness is the very heart of his Godhood. Even when God saves sinners from their sins—a supreme act of generosity— God insists that he's doing it for his own benefit more than for ours. What's God's perspective on his saving us? Observe how he speaks of salvation:

> For my own sake, for my own sake, I do this.
>   How can I let myself be defamed?
>   I will not yield my glory to another. (Is 48:11)

Now I have another secret. Some time ago I taught at a youth retreat. (That's not the secret part.) I was surprised afterward when they paid me for speaking. So I wondered, *What would be the most appropriate use for money from a Christian youth retreat?* I chewed over it for some time and then it popped into my head: *I'll go get tattooed!* So off I went to have Isaiah 48:11 tattooed around my ankle in Greek from the Septuagint.

It felt sort of like running my leg through a sewing machine—for half an hour. Folks, if you're under eighteen, don't do this. And if you're over eighteen, think long and hard first. I won't know for sure whether God likes my tattoo until I get resurrected and look at my ankle. Still, I like to think of it as a little "note to self": "Dear self. God has decided not to share his glory with you today. He wants it all for himself. Your Friend,

Greg." Tattoo or no, the point is clear: God rescues us not because of anything in us but because we bear his name, which he doesn't want disrespected. We were made to glorify God. To glorify God means to display his greatness, to put his perfections on show, to further his fame.

The selfishness of God is the foundation for our existence and the reason we can seek him for blessing. David prayed for forgiveness, saying, "For the sake of your name, O LORD, forgive my iniquity, though it is great" (Ps 25:11). The Holy Spirit's ministry on earth is to bring glory to Jesus (Jn 16:14), and Jesus is coming back at the end of the age "to be glorified in his holy people and to be marveled at among all those who have believed" (2 Thess 1:9-10). All this so that the knowledge of God's glory can fill the earth as the waters cover the sea (Hab 2:14). The religion of the Bible is about God and his fame. What does that make us? A means to an end.

What an End!

About A.D. 400 Aurelius Augustine, the greatest theological mind in the early church, clarified this point well. Everything, Augustine explained, is either an instrument or an end. Instruments have a purpose beyond themselves. A pencil is an instrument for writing; a painting an instrument to display beauty. Instruments are properly used for other ends. God alone is not an instrument, Augustine argued, but the end for which everything else exists.

What? Even human beings? Is a person just a means, something to be used?

Yes, though not by other people, only by God. To deny this puts yourself in the serpent's shoes. When the best theologians of the seventeenth century developed a teaching tool for children and new believers, this was their first point. The opening question of the *Westminster Shorter Catechism* asks, "What is the chief end of man?" That is, what's our purpose? Why are we here?

The answer? "Man's chief end is to glorify God, and to enjoy him forever." We exist to display God's character, to glorify him. A passion for God's glory is the Christian's highest motivation and uppermost principle guiding his or her life. "So whether you eat or drink or whatever you do, do it all for the glory of God" (1 Cor 10:31). The English revivalist was known to have cried, "Let the name of Whitefield perish, so long as God is glorified!"

I'm convinced that understanding God's supremacy brings us not bondage but freedom. Only when meaning is sought beyond the limits of this world is significance found within it. Yes, we are means to an end. But what an end! To be valuable to the Almighty as a vehicle by which he is glorified—there is nothing greater.

The satisfaction for our souls, our very significance as creatures lie in God's glory. As a pencil longs to write and a shovel to dig, so our hearts long for God. We find joy in our purpose. Only as humble creatures before him do we find life. Ecclesiastes teaches that by itself everything on this earth is meaningless. Jesus wasn't joking when he said, "Whoever loses his life for my sake will find it" (Mt 10:39).

As the Westminster divines expressed, joy goes hand in hand with glorifying God. We were made to glorify God *and to enjoy him forever*—two sides of the same coin. They didn't ask about our chief *ends*, but *end*—one purpose with two facets. God is the source of our joy, and as we bring him glory, we enjoy him as the one for whom we were created.

A heart that's radically committed to bringing God glory is a heart full of joy in him. C. S. Lewis wasn't the first Christian "surprised by joy" after turning to God. In his *Confessions*, a book-length prayer to God, Augustine cried out to his Maker:

> To praise you is the desire of man, a little piece of your creation. You stir man to take pleasure in praising you, because you have made us for yourself, and our heart is restless until it rests in you.[1]

By finding our satisfaction in God we join the psalmist:

> My soul yearns, even faints,
>   for the courts of the LORD;

---

[1]Augustine, *Confessions*, trans. Henry Chadwick (Oxford: Oxford University Press, 1991), p. 3.

> *my heart and my flesh cry out*
> *for the living God. (Ps 84:2)*

We come to glorify God not in an abstract way but in a relationship. We were made to know God, a knowledge that Moses prayed for (Ex 33:13), that Jesus called eternal life (Jn 17:3), that will spread to the ends of the earth under Messiah's reign (Jer 31:34). Our significance, joy and relationship with God all derive from our high calling of bringing glory, honor and praise to God.

The Image of God: A High Self-Image

Christianity is far more humanistic than the humanism of the last century. To turn your back on God is not to find your humanity but to lose it. God has made us his image. God's image is the dividing line between human and animal. From the beginning the image of God makes us creatures of dignity, value and worth.

> *Then God said, "Let us make man in our image, in our likeness, and let them rule over the fish of the sea and the birds of the air, over the livestock, over all the earth, and over all the creatures that move along the ground."*
> *So God created man in his own image, in the image of God he created him; male and female he created them. (Gen 1:26-27)*

What does this mean? To be an image of God—at the bare minimum—means to be *like God* in some respects, and to *represent* God. In what ways are we like God?

We see God creating humans with *knowledge and rationality,* surpassing that of the animals, reflecting in some measure the wisdom of God. God speaks to his human creatures using language. He calls upon Adam to name or classify the animals—a task reflecting God's creative power. God could have named them himself, but he makes humanity cocreators—albeit in a small way. God's image images God's *creativity.* And Adam reflects God's *righteousness and holiness* at creation—being declared very good, not yet knowing sin. And he is given a test the animals never received—a command not to eat from the tree in the middle of the Garden.

Dominion is also part of God's image. God commissions the first humans to exercise his rule on his behalf to "fill the earth and subdue it." He continues, emphasizing the kingly quality, "Rule over the fish of the sea and the birds of the air and over every living creature that moves on the ground" (Gen 1:28). Look at the forests and the beasts. You are God's representative to the other species.

The psalmist expresses wonder at the place of honor God gives us.

What is man that you are mindful of him? . . .
You made him a little lower than the heavenly beings
and crowned him with glory and honor.
You made him ruler over the works of your hands;
you put everything under his feet. (Ps 8:4-6)

The human calling is no lowly endeavor. In making you his ambassador to creation God has placed upon your head a crown of glory. Dominion over nature is a vital facet of bearing God's image.

Being God's image also entails a corporate life—*community*. We see God's corporate nature immediately. "Let us make man in our image, in our likeness," he says (Gen 1:26). God created us "male and female" in the image of God (Gen 1:27). This doesn't mean we only recognize our full human potential in marriage, as some have suggested. Jesus was "the very image of God" but remained unmarried, as did his apostle Paul. Still, God's communal nature as a Trinity is, in part, reflected in his image through our relational nature.

All humans form societies, families, friendships. Relationships are an essential part of our humanness. No wonder that when God saves people from sin, he never does so in an individualistic manner. Rather, he incorporates them into a church, a community of God. But even before sin God says, "It is not good for the man to be alone" (Gen 2:18). God's image—the sole factor that separates us from other animals—is what makes us like God. In this image we reflect God's knowledge, creativity, righteousness, dominion and community. We're invested with a high significance as God's representatives to the earth.

This divine image, though defiled by our sin, has not been removed.

After the flood God instituted the death penalty for murder. Why? "For in the image of God / has God made man" (Gen 9:6). To shed human blood is to kill God in effigy—a crime God considers worthy of the greatest punishment, to lose what is most valuable in creation—human life itself.

Such a penalty speaks not to a low view of humanity but an incredibly high one. It speaks to the sanctity of human life as the image of God. Thus, James can bemoan the way we attack God's image with our speech. "With the tongue we praise our Lord and Father, and with it we curse men, who have been made in God's likeness" (Jas 3:9).

As one who is like God, who represents God to the world, you have a dignity higher than any other creature, a high and noble calling. Every one of us demonstrates God's knowledge, creativity, righteousness, dominion and community to some degree. Even the unborn baby, developmentally disabled child and comatose person bear God's image and are worthy of our reverence and protection as creatures of dignity before God. People's lives aren't precious because they're self-sufficient or have something to offer society, but because as God's image they're sacred. Sadly, though, the story doesn't end with our creation in God's image.

The Image Defiled: A Low Self-Image

So long as people are creatures, our significance depends upon God's ultimate significance. And since our value is derived, it can be diminished as his image in us is defiled. Some theologians have stressed the high self-image all people should have as God's image bearers. But to ignore the devastating effects of sin is just as flawed as ignoring the divine image that remains even in the sinner.

Imagine one of those antique shows on television. A lady presents her mahogany china cabinet to the expert from Sotheby's. After much interrogation he tells her it's not a forgery. It's an authentic eighteenth-century New England cabinet. The viewers pull closer to hear its value. "Were it in perfect condition, this piece could fetch anywhere from eighty to one-hundred thousand dollars."

Wow!

"But," he adds, "this piece is not in very good shape. It's been refinished several times, and the original hardware is missing. Further, the fine detailing is all but ruined, and the top half is much later than the bottom—say, 1950s." Ooh. This is bad. "I'd estimate its value at about fifteen hundred dollars." Granted, fifteen hundred dollars is still a lot of money, but it's such a loss compared to what it once was.

I'm afraid we're a lot like this china cabinet. Sin has defaced God's image. It is still there in a structural sense, but it's a ruined image. Rationality? People today are more driven by feeling than thinking. Creativity? Yes, but often harnessed toward ungodly ends. Righteousness? No comment needed. Dominion? Nature is in rebellion; we've exercised dominion very, very poorly. And community? We live in a world of terribly lonely people and our repeatedly damaged relationships.

But should sin affect our self-image? It certainly affects how God sees us. When the Israelites rejected God's covenant, "they followed worthless idols and themselves became worthless" (2 Kings 17:15). God repeats this assessment in Jeremiah 2:5 and Hosea 12:11. Before the infinite God all who live in rebellion against God are called "worthless and less than nothing" (Is 40:17). Sin's nature is to defile us (Ezek 20:43), to rob us of our humanity. Paul concludes that sinful humanity had become worthless in the eyes of the Lord (Rom 3:12). Perhaps these passages use hyperbole—overstatement for rhetorical effect. Nevertheless, God says that sin cheapens our humanity and robs us of our dignity.

God shows tremendous love for all people, believers and unbelievers alike, as his own image. Yet a holy hatred flows alongside such tremendous love. When God considers wicked and defiled humanity, he finds them repulsive:

> *The arrogant cannot stand in your presence;*
> *you hate all who do wrong.*
> *You destroy those who tell lies;*
> *bloodthirsty and deceitful men*
> *the LORD abhors. (Ps 5:5-6)*

Sin's defilement allows no separation of sin and sinner. When God redeems, it is the *whole person* that he redeems, making us new creatures in Christ (2 Cor 5:17). But just as surely, when God judges and condemns, his sentence rests upon the whole person—sin and defiled soul. God is completely opposed to evil and all its effects. Job's reaction to his sin when contrasted with God's greatness was surely appropriate, "Therefore I despise myself / and repent in dust and ashes" (Job 42:6).

James counsels unrepentant readers, "Grieve, mourn and wail. Change your laughter to mourning and your joy to gloom" (Jas 4:9). We have spoiled God's image, and the stains run deep. Such devastation is truly a cause for mourning. By turning our souls from the God we image, we have cheapened our very humanness.

The Image Being Restored: An Accurate Self-Image

For those who remain outside of Christ, the story is tragic. Divorced from him who is beauty himself, the soul at war with God can only grow uglier. But when God invades a heart with faith, uniting that person with Jesus Christ, the decline reverses. "Therefore, if anyone is in Christ, he is a new creation; the old has gone, the new has come" (2 Cor 5:17).

The progress of the Christian life—what is usually called sanctification—is God's restoration of the damaged image. I've been amazed to follow the restoration of Leonardo da Vinci's famous mural *The Last Supper*. As experts have painstakingly removed centuries of grime, the entire picture has changed. Lines that were covered become visible; facial expressions that were missing can be seen. The colors are radically different. Gone are the dark, smoky forms. It's bright and bold. The original has been restored.

If you wonder what's going on inside as you live by faith in Jesus, realize God is at work. And he's making you what he designed you to be as his image and likeness. He's restoring that image, making you again into what you truly are. We "are being transformed into his likeness with ever-increasing glory" (2 Cor 3:18). In Jesus, you "have put on the new self, which is being renewed in knowledge in the image of its Creator" (Col 3:9-11). Image restoration is God's purpose. Our Father "predestined us to be conformed to the likeness of his Son" (Rom 8:29).

When Jesus returns to earth in glory, "We shall be like him" (1 Jn 3:2). We'll image God more fully than Adam did, for we'll be the likeness of the man from heaven, Christ the Lord (1 Cor 15:49). God has committed himself eternally to fix what we messed up, to reverse the effects of sin, remove centuries of grime, and reveal the splendor that lies in union with Christ just under the surface.

So how should we think about ourselves? Should we think only positive thoughts? Should we speak to ourselves about our infinite worth? We'd be living a lie if we did. Should we instead bemoan our sinfulness and wallow in self-hatred? No, that would bring into doubt the goodness of our creator and redeemer God. The Christian view of people—people according to God—takes into account both the glory and the shame of being human.

Part of the problem with so much talk about self-image and self-esteem is that we're asking the wrong question. *Perhaps we spend too much time thinking about ourselves to begin with.* Maybe the real problem is our introspection, our bending inward on ourselves. Our creatureliness calls us not to spend so much time thinking about ourselves. Self-loathing is just as self-focused as pride. As relational beings, our hearts find their satisfaction, not in ourselves, but in relationship with God and neighbor. Our Father calls us repeatedly to move our eyes off ourselves and our foul condition and to meditate upon his perfections and promises.

Still, it's naive to think we should have no self-image of any kind. So what do we conclude? Scripture sometimes tells us to lower our views of ourselves; at other times it affirms truly lofty assessments about us.

The human person is a multifaceted jewel. You should grieve your brokenness in sin. But you should rejoice that your true self is your new self. That's high. God's total commitment to you as a redeemed child is cause for confidence, not timidity.

But you still sin in word, thought and deed. I take the Bible's word for it. My character remains full of sin, self-aggrandizement and deceit. You and I bear God's image, an image being restored. At the same time, however, we are but creatures, means to the end of glorifying God. Then again, what an end! Take Paul's words to heart and focus on developing an *accurate* self-image:

> *For by the grace given me, I say to every one of you: Do not think of yourself more highly than you ought, but rather think of yourself with sober judgment, in accordance with the measure of faith God has given you. (Rom 12:3)*

Knowing God's unshakable love for us as his people, we're free to enter honestly into a sober self-assessment of our character—without getting stuck on ourselves. What do I love? What do I hate? What do I do when no one else is watching? But when we fail, we don't have to wallow in self-pity. We're just being the fallen creatures we are. And it shouldn't surprise us when others fail us either. A boss who explodes every time an employee drops the ball doesn't understand his own weaknesses, let alone the weaknesses of others. A woman who judges her spouse for not being perfect hasn't understood what it means to be human after the Fall.

At the same time, a person who despairs of ever doing anything right also hasn't grasped the full import of being human. We are God's image, albeit a shattered image. And in Christ we can rise above mediocrity to pursue excellence—even though God's grace may move us toward it one baby step at a time.

Knowing that people are God's image—and therefore valuable to him—our hearts should long to care for the needs of others. And realizing the brokenness that sin has caused, we don't naively expect those we love always to reciprocate. God's restoration of his image in us through Christ provides the most powerful motive possible to love other people. Receiving grace enables us to give grace. As we begin delighting in God for God's sake, so we begin delighting in God's image in our neighbor. When God turns our hearts toward him, we become less preoccupied with ourselves and can care for others in quiet but concrete ways. Not so that we'll receive accolades, but because God is restoring us to be what he intended—people who love one another as a concrete display of God's glory.

Having a biblical understanding of people—of our weaknesses as well as our strengths—we can enter with a realistic mindset into the life God designed for us. We enter into this pattern of life imperfectly, bringing our brokenness with us. But enter we do, with the full expectation that we'll find joy as we glorify God in the many spheres of life he's prepared for us. We take up this calling not because we know how great we are as humans. We do so because we know how great the God is who made us, called us and empowers us to change the world that he created.

Questions for Discussion

1. Why do you think it's so difficult to answer the question "Should we think highly or lowly of ourselves?"

2. How would you answer someone asking, "Why did God need to create us?" How does a better understanding of God and his purposes help us better understand ourselves and our purposes?

3. The *Westminster Shorter Catechism* says that man's chief end (our primary purpose) is to glorify and enjoy God. How does this lower our view of ourselves? How does it raise our view of ourselves?

4. In your own words, what does it mean to be an image of God? In what ways has sin affected God's image in us?

5. A friend objects, "I can't deny myself to follow Christ—I've only recently found myself!" How might you respond?

6. How should a believer view himself differently from an unbeliever? How does God view them differently? What difference does faith in Christ make for your humanity?

7. Salvation in Christ is about more than just forgiveness, more than "getting saved"—how has this chapter developed this theme?

4

THE LAW IN NATURE

Authority According to God

"And God blessed the seventh day and made it holy."
GENESIS 2:3

Authority is a contentious issue, perhaps because this concept is so closely intertwined with the concept of law. Among Christians certain recurring issues always cause disagreement. One is the role God's law plays in the believer's life. Paul does, after all, repeat many times that we are not under law but under grace (Rom 6:14-15).

But Paul doesn't mean that God's law is no longer our guide in living. Rather, he means we are free from the *condemnation* of the law through Jesus Christ (Rom 8:1-4). God's enemies refuse to submit to his instruction, not his children. Paul explains: "The sinful mind is hostile to God. It does not submit to God's law, nor can it do so" (Rom 8:7). The law is good if used properly (1 Tim 1:8). The believing heart sees God's law as his friend (Ps 119:97). Though certain Old Testament commands have been fulfilled by Jesus Christ (Mt 5:17), God's law remains our final authority.

When we speak of God's law in this sense, we aren't usually speaking of the whole of the Scripture, nor do we even mean the Mosaic code expressed in Leviticus and Deuteronomy. God's law refers to his moral standard of right and wrong, the loving principles given as the moral pattern for all people in all places, at all times. This law never changes; it is the expression of his unchanging character (1 Sam 15:29; Jas 1:17). What God loves is good; what God hates is sin. His law reveals God's heart.

The moral standards of the Old and New Testaments speak with one voice: love him with all my heart, soul, mind and strength and love my neighbor as myself. These Jesus called the greatest commandments (Mk 12:28-31). But these were the law in Moses' day too—Jesus was quoting word-for-word from Deuteronomy 6:4-5 and Leviticus 19:18. Indeed, Jesus claimed that the obligation to God first and neighbor second was the central moral thrust of everything God has told us (Mt 22:40).

These two commands are the structure behind the Ten Commandments (Ex 20). The first four explain how to love God; the latter six tell us how to love our neighbors. The rest of the case law in Exodus, Leviticus, Numbers and Deuteronomy merely illustrates these core moral principles in various contexts, adding civil penalties for the state of Israel.

But few evangelicals even know the Ten Commandments. I saw that myself in a congregation of several thousand. I suspect this is a compromise with our culture. We live in a lawless age. Over half of Americans say they'll cheat on their spouses, almost a third admit to cheating on their taxes, and half say they'll do absolutely nothing at work about one day in five.[1] In the name of personal freedom and choice (the politically correct translation of *lawlessness*), Americans kill over a million unborn babies a year. Lawlessness abounds.

What's tragic is the degree to which this attitude has infiltrated the churches. I'm particularly concerned about the lack of respect toward church leaders. The Bible tells us to submit to our church leaders and obey them (Heb 13:17), but we more often undermine them through criticism, complaining or factions. Then when that fails, we withdraw—our money, our encouragement or our presence.

---

[1]James Patterson and Peter Kim, *The Day America Told the Truth* (New York: Plume, 1992), p. 201.

The way we disrespect authorities God puts over us is another form of lawlessness. Think of all the disrespectful jokes and comments told about people in authority. Christ's message was sometimes harsh toward those who abused their authority, but he never brought authority into question.

Our whole attitude needs a major adjustment. Submission and obedience have become dirty words. We hear many sermons on faith. How many have you heard about obedience? Submission? "Trust and obey, for there's no other way" has been shortened in the contemporary church.

God's law is a "perfect law that gives freedom" to those who live by it (Jas 1:25). While we belong to God by grace through faith in Jesus Christ, we only know *what it looks like* to trust God day by day from his commandments. God redeems us, not to ignore his law, but to fulfill it (Rom 13:10). Law shows us how to live by faith under authority.

Authority and Law in God's Design for Creation

Authority, at its most basic level, is the right and responsibility to lead in a certain situation. Ultimate authority rests in God alone and, in this era, specifically in Jesus Christ (Mt 28:18).

Human authority is derived from and dependent upon him. "There is no authority except that which God has established. The authorities that exist have been established by God" (Rom 13:1). Though Paul wrote this when the emperor, Nero, was abusing his authority by killing Christians, the apostle nevertheless insists that the authorities receive their right to exercise power from God. The authority itself is legitimate, even if their abuse isn't.

Of course, sometimes human authorities must be respectfully disobeyed in order to honor God—like when we're commanded to sin by action or inaction (Acts 4:18-20). I once had to disobey an employer who commanded me to sell laughing gas canisters (a.k.a. whipped cream chargers) to children. But I still respected my boss's authority even when disobeying him in order to be faithful to God.

In the last chapter we considered how God designed our relationship with him to display his glory. But our relationship with God is not our only authority-based relationship. He's placed us in a whole web of authority relationships; they're in the very fabric of God's creation. Marriage and family, government, culture, work, science and education are all spheres of life God established in the beginning. Each of these spheres involve authority relationships of different kinds.

This doesn't mean all people with power have authority—authority and power are different. Power may or may not be legitimate—the guy who broke into my Honda and stole my *Saturday Night Fever* soundtrack had power but no authority. The policemen who arrested the guy had authority as well as power. They had the right to direct the affairs of other people within the limitations of their sphere.

Scripture repeatedly concerns itself with relationships, including authority relationships. After Paul speaks of submission in Ephesians, he continues to illustrate humble leadership and submission in various authority relationships, instructing wives and husbands, children and parents, then slaves and masters (Eph 5:21—6:9). Peter uses the same pattern (1 Pet 2:13—3:7). The biblical authors speak grace into all these authority relationships.

Certainly we see the effects of the Fall in all of these relationships. Jesus reversed the prideful pattern of this world when he taught us to do as he himself did—to serve when we lead, to put the needs of those under our authority above our own.

> *"You know that the rulers of the Gentiles lord it over them, and their high officials exercise authority over them. Not so with you. Instead, whoever wants to become great among you must be your servant, and whoever wants to be first must be your slave—just as the Son of Man did not come to be served, but to serve, and to give his life as a ransom for many." (Mt 20:25-28)*

Jesus wasn't rejecting all authority. But he challenged his followers to give themselves like he did. Jesus, who had all authority, gave himself to humiliation and death for his subjects.

Faithful exercise of authority is regulated by God's loving instruction—his law. Just as God's law structures our relationship with him in Christ, so also God's law structures the various spheres of life he gave at creation. God's law is the foundation for orderly life on planet earth.

Law in Creation

But what about people who lived before the Bible was written? If they didn't have God's law written down for them, how did Adam and Eve know right from wrong? Before God gave us his Son or even his Scriptures, his law was clearly written within the fabric of creation. Nature is God's first book, and within it he revealed his law—his moral instruction. Paul explains, "Indeed, when the Gentiles who do not have the law, do *by nature* things required by the law . . . they show that the requirements of the law are written on their hearts" (Rom 2:14-15, emphasis mine).

Paul lists about twenty-two specific sins that everybody instinctively knows offend God, even though we still commit them, even encouraging others to do the same (Rom 1:27-32). Even in humanity's rebellion, God still makes sure people know his law. He restrains sinners from being as bad as they could be. Some theologians call this divine protection *common grace* because it's common to all people.

When we consider the good nature God gave humanity at creation, sin is truly unnatural. For example, homosexual sin is wrong, Paul says, not simply because it violates the proscription of Leviticus 18:22 (which it does), but because it's against *nature* (Rom 1:26-27). Paul could have said this about any sin. We weren't made for sin.

Even if we distort, disregard or disobey God's law, we still know right and wrong deep down inside—people who don't seem to know it are called sociopaths. The Chinese philosopher Confucius said not to do to someone else what you wouldn't want them doing to you (the "Silver Rule"). Confucius didn't get this from Jesus or a Bible. Rather, this moral wisdom—what is traditionally called *natural law*—was written into the natural world and upon the human heart from the beginning.

We see natural law at work with the establishment of the sabbath day of rest at creation. "And God blessed the seventh day and made it holy, because on it he rested from all the work of creating that he had done" (Gen 2:3). The Israelites didn't receive the sabbath command *in writing* until Moses brought it down from Sinai (Ex 20:8-11), but the principle was there from creation.

Still, the Israelites knew the command before it was written; they rested on the sabbath before ever reaching Sinai (Ex 16:23, 29-30). And the sabbath continues in principle in the New Testament as the first day of the week, the Lord's Day (Acts 20:7; 1 Cor 16:1-2; Rev 1:10).

Every sphere of life—whether government, industry, the family or education—lives under God's law, which is written on every heart and restated in Scripture. And every sphere of life involves authority. Yet authority raises a lot of issues, which we need to understand in their true perspective according to God.

Authority in God's Design for Men and Women

Whenever I teach on the differing authority roles of women and men, I've found that no matter what I say, some people call me a feminist while others call me a patriarchal reactionary. Given the certain criticism, I'll try to stick close to the Bible and take into account all—not just half—the biblical data. And I'll attempt to do so without relativizing the biblical passages that seem to rub me the wrong way.

When the Bible talks about men, women and authority, two major principles resurface at every turn. First, *men and women are equal*. Second, *men and women are different*. And some authority functions God reserves for men.

The Equality of Women and Men According to God

When I taught at a Baptist seminary in eastern Ukraine, I really had to stress this biblical equality of the sexes. While under Soviet rule women and men were officially equal, Russian society has always treated women poorly. Further, many Baptists had overreacted to the liberal trends of the past century by severely limiting the activities allowed women. But Russians like lists. So I came up with a list showing ways God says men and women are equal.

Women and men equally bear God's image (Gen 1:27) and are equally united to Jesus Christ through faith (Gal 3:26-29). Women have the same responsibility to obey God's law (Ex 20), and to teach it (Deut 6:6-7; Prov 6:20). Women have the same access to God as men, as seen in the lives of remarkable women like Hagar (Gen 16:8-13) and Samson's mother (Judg 13:2-5).

Women have always had vital roles of ministry and respect among God's people. Women, like men, were prophets of God in both testaments: Huldah (2 Kings 22:14-20), Miriam (Ex 15:20) and Philip's daughters (Acts 21:9). They served at the tabernacle entrance (Ex 38:8), and provided significant ministries within the church. Priscilla, for example, taught Apollos alongside her husband (Acts 18:26). And women receive as much recognition in the church for their service as do men (Rom 16:1-15). Jesus' ministry was funded largely by a group of women who supported him out of their own means (Lk 8:1-3).

And within society at large, women, like men, could serve in public office. God raised up Deborah to rule the nation of Israel (Judg 4:1—5:31). I'd be thrilled to call a God-fearing sister in Christ Madam President. And God calls women, like men, to engage freely in commerce and business.

She considers a field and buys it;
  out of her own earnings she plants a vineyard.
She sets about her work vigorously;
  her arms are strong for her tasks.
She sees that her trading is profitable,
  and her lamp does not go out at night. . . .
She is clothed with strength and dignity;
  she can laugh at the days to come.
She speaks with wisdom,
  and faithful instruction is on her tongue. (Prov 31:16-18, 25-26)

This woman makes major decisions, is trusted with finances, has dignity and gives instruction. Yet this is not a self-made woman; her foundation is the fear of the Lord (Prov 31:30). Lydia was such a woman in the early church (Acts 16:14-15).

The women in my class in Ukraine were thrilled with this teaching. But I hadn't gotten halfway through before some men objected, "What about submission?! What about 1 Timothy 2?!" "That's second," I answered, "We have to get first things first."

It's not an exaggeration to say that the Christians were the feminists of the ancient world. The Greek philosophers considered women to be deformed men, and the culture of antiquity provided women few rights. According to a rabbinic saying it was better to teach a dog than a woman.

Jesus flagrantly defied the sexism of his culture: teaching women, speaking to women, even developing personal friendships with women (Jn 11:5). Jesus' association with women surprised even his disciples (Jn 4:27). Not until Rome had its first Christian emperor—Constantine—were women legally permitted to remain single.

It could be said that modern feminism—despite its often anti-Christian rhetoric—could only have arisen in a culture heavily influenced by the followers of Jesus Christ. I doubt feminism could have arisen in Hindu India, where widows were encouraged to throw themselves upon their husbands' funeral pyres and burn to death. Nor in the Muslim world, where in some parts women are still kept behind veils. The dignity of women was first championed by Jesus and his people.

If I stopped at this point, many readers might think me an evangelical feminist. While I appreciate feminists' emphasis on the equality of the sexes, I am also convinced that God-given differences between women and men impact our functions in the family and, to some extent, the church.

In Ukraine I taught that the sexes were equal but different, and they were uneasy with the equality. In the United States I teach the same, and people accuse me of sexism. Every culture on planet Earth has its own value system. But we can't accept *any* of these—not even the American one. If we're going to see the world according to God, then we have to reject the world's categories in favor of God's categories.

The Differences According to God

God designed us distinctly to be either men or women. Men and women are different, and because of these differences of design God reserves a couple authority functions for men. Equality does not mean interchangeability. God has a different design for each.

Any talk about differing roles for men and women tends to cause as much confusion as it does clarity. When we talk about different roles, we tend to get a picture of women cooking, vacuuming, cleaning the toilets and staying home with the kids while the men go play pool with their buddies. Please wipe that picture from your mind. The *Leave It to Beaver* vision isn't necessarily what God has in mind.

It's obvious to most people that men and women are different. But what's not always so obvious is that these differences penetrate deep below the surface. Men and women think differently and have different strengths and weaknesses. I recently read about a study that scanned people's brains as they listened to different sounds. They found that women hear with both sides of their brains, while men only hear with one side. The researchers cautioned that they couldn't prove that men don't listen as well, only that men and women listen differently. (Did you say something?)

Scripture speaks to the origin of these differences.

> *But for Adam no suitable helper was found. So the LORD God caused the man to fall into a deep sleep; and while he was sleeping, he took one of the man's ribs and closed up the place with flesh. Then the LORD God made a woman from the rib he had taken out of the man, and he brought her to the man.*
> *The man said,*
> > *"This is now bone of my bone*
> > *and flesh of my flesh;*
> > *she shall be called 'woman,'*
> > *for she was taken out of man." (Gen 2:20-23)*

This passage continues with God establishing marriage (Gen 2:24).

Within this partnership of equals, the man was given a function of providing leadership. Consider how Paul uses this passage in the New Testament: "Now I want to realize that the head of every man is Christ, and the head of the woman is man, and the head of Christ is God" (1 Cor 11:3). Three authority relationships are in view: the Father over the Son, the Son over the man and the man over his wife. But why does Paul identify the husband as having the authority (headship) in the family? He refers to the order of creation, "For man did not come from woman, but woman from man; neither was man created for woman, but woman for man" (1 Cor 11:8-9). According to the apostle, male headship is not a curse of the Fall but a gift of creation.

The woman was made with the function of *helper*. German theologian Werner Neuer writes, "The man according to Genesis 2:18 is the origin and goal of the woman. Woman is taken out of man and created for him to complete him and to help him. This relationship is not reversible."[2] Male headship within the family—and the completing support position of the wife—are evident from the very beginning. But helping isn't necessarily a demeaning function—God himself is called Israel's *helper* (*ezer*, the same term) fifteen times in Scripture.

In her critique of evangelical feminism Susan Foh reminds us that this vision was one untainted by human sin:

> *God's assignment of functions may sound like job discrimination to us. . . .*
> *We feel a twinge (or maybe a pang) of resentment because we do not know what a sin-free hierarchical arrangement can be like. We know only the arbitrariness, the domination, the arrogance that even the best boss/underling relationship has. But in Eden, it was different. It really was. The man and the woman knew each other as equals, both in the image of God, and thus each with a personal relationship to God. Neither doubted the worth of the other. . . .*
> *Each was to perform his/her task in a different way, the man as the head and the woman as his helper. They operated as truly one flesh, one person.*[3]

God designed the woman to be man's complement. Using the *yin and yang* illustration (think Korean flag) may be criticized as non-Christian imagery. But when it comes to marriage, it fits. The two halves of the circle are different, but fit together to make the whole.

Consider these comments on Eve's creation from Adam's rib, by the English Puritan Matthew Henry nearly three centuries before modern feminism:

> *That the woman was made of a rib out of the side of Adam; not made out of*

---

[2]Werner Neuer, *Man and Woman in Christian Perspective*, trans. Gordon J. Wenham (Wheaton, Ill.: Crossway, 1991), p. 73.
[3]Susan T. Foh, *Women and the Word of God: A Response to Biblical Feminism* (Phillipsburg, N.J.: Presbyterian & Reformed, 1979), p. 62.

> *his head to rule over him, nor out of his feet to be trampled upon by him, but*
> *out of his side to be equal to him, under his arm to be protected, and near his*
> *heart to be beloved.*[4]

Equal, he writes, yet protected by her husband. As head, Adam was to guide the family, which he failed to do from the start. Rather than leading his wife away from sin, he followed her into it. God's judgment upon Adam starts "Because you listened to your wife" (Gen 3:17). Adam's sin was a sin of silence, a failure to lead. He listened to his wife when he should have been leading her away from danger. He was passive when he should have been active. He failed to take responsibility and willingly let himself and his wife be led into sin.

Since Adam had the responsibility to lead—not Eve—it was Adam God summoned after the Fall (Gen 3:9). And even though Eve ate the forbidden fruit first, Adam receives the blame for it throughout Scripture (Rom 5:12-14). The husband as head of his wife means he carries God's authority—and responsibility—to humbly lead his family as a servant (Eph 5:23).

Within the home God calls married women to respect, honor and submit to their husband's authority. "Wives, in the same way be submissive to your husbands" (1 Pet 3:1). This isn't merely because the ancient world expected submission, a passing cultural fad. No, God grounds his reason in creation itself, "For man did not come from woman, but woman from man; neither was man created for woman, but woman for man" (1 Cor 11:8-9). God's order for the family is a universal creation ordinance.

But notice that Paul's command "submit to your husbands as to the Lord" (Eph 5:22), is not for all women to submit to all men. It's about wives each being submissive to their husbands rather than usurping their responsibility to provide leadership. These passages don't speak to society or the workplace, but a particular authority relationship between husband and wife.

---

[4]Matthew Henry, *Commentary on the Whole Bible*, ed. Leslie F. Church (Grand Rapids, Mich.: Zondervan, 1961), p. 7.

But what about the men? As God calls wives to pour themselves into their husbands out of service to Christ, God calls husbands to give up their lives out of love for their wives. "Husbands, love your wives, just as Christ loved the church and gave himself up for her to make her holy" (Eph 5:25-26). If the wife's calling is to find life by submitting, the husband's is to find life by dying. There's no room here for men to abuse God's design for submission if their call is to slay their own desires in dependence on God and love for their families.

The key is that neither the husband's nor the wife's calling comes because their spouses are worthy in themselves. Wives submit "as to the Lord," as a ministry to Jesus, their worthy Lord. Similarly, husbands love enough to die for the sake of leadership, not because their wives are always lovable but because Jesus gives the example, dying while we were an unfaithful wife at best.

The husband, if he really understands what God has called him to, has every bit as hard a function as his wife. Both husband and wife have to give up what they want—they both live in mutual submission to God and each other (Eph 5:21). And a godly wife is the husband's chief counselor. What man would be so blinded as to refuse the advice of the helper God provides him? Husband and wife make decisions together, both giving up their own self-interest to follow God's leading. But when push comes to shove and a couple can't determine which way God is leading, then it's the husband who will give account for the direction taken. Of course, if he leads the family into sin, a wife may have to respectfully tell him, "I must obey God rather than men" (Acts 4:19).

But when spouses can't reach agreement and either possibility is good, then God's structure of headship should be honored. The husband should lead in sacrifice, considering his wife's happiness before his own. But if he's convinced of God's leading, his wife should support him— even if she believes another path is better. The alternative—husband and wife heading down different paths—is not God's best for the family.

But what if the path chosen was a bad one? What happens when the investments you made loose all their value or the house you purchased falls apart? Thankfully, God is great enough—even in the wake of our failures—to provide for and restore families after the leader took an unwise direction.

Within marriage, husband and wife are equal, but not interchangeable. Both are noble callings. The servant-leader and the helper-supporter work hand in hand, complementing one another. "In the Lord, however, woman is not independent of man, nor is man independent of woman. For as woman came from man, so also man is born of woman. But everything comes from God" (1 Cor 11:11-12). God's design has balance; each is given to the other to complete the whole that is the Christian family.

In the Church: The Apostolic Injunction

Within the church—the family of God—the same principles operate. Women are central to the ministry of the church—Phoebe was a servant (or possibly a deaconess) of the church at Cenchrea (Rom 16:1). Indeed, half the people Paul greets at the end of Romans were women. Women could prophesy in the New Testament church, as did Philip's daughters (Acts 21:9). They could also teach—Priscilla even teaching an apostle like Apollos with her husband Aquilla (Acts 18:26).

Given the prominent ministry women enjoyed, it would be tempting to assume there were no differences in the roles of men and women in the New Testament church. But that would be a mistake. To relegate the rest of the biblical data to the category of *exceptions* or *culturally conditioned passages* is not sound theological method. All of the Scriptures are inspired by God, even if they offend our modern feministic sensibilities

Alongside this significant place of women in New Testament ministry, we also see a gender distinction in at least one specific office, that of elder, the chief pastoral and leadership office in the early church.

Speaking of the authoritative teaching office of elder, Paul states with apostolic authority, "I do not allow a woman to teach or to have authority over a man; she must be silent" (1 Tim 2:12). Paul wasn't speaking generally here. He wrote these words in a discussion about organized public worship prior to listing the qualifications for the office of elder. The teaching Paul had in mind was likely preaching, and the authority he probably meant was the leadership office of elder. Still, his words are strong ones, using the language of universal prohibition.

For nineteen centuries the universal practice of the Christian church has been to restrict this office—whatever it has been called—to men. Many have sought to change this practice in recent years. Some have capitalized on Paul's use of the first person "I" to suggest this may have been a temporary injunction reflecting Paul's will and not God's. But that would not be a sound reading.

Others have suggested this was simply a temporary injunction against women pastors on account of the misogyny of Greek culture, that is, since women are disrespected by pagans, we shouldn't let them have positions of leadership yet. But again, this is not what the text says. Yet others argue this was a temporary regulation to allow women the time to educate themselves properly for the office. However, Paul gives his reason, and it was not the misogyny of Greek culture, nor women's lack of education (a historical fiction), nor a personal thing on Paul's part. What was his reasoning?

When we look at the New Testament, there are passages where the instruction is culturally conditioned. How can you know? While Christians will not always agree, if the instruction was given to address a specific need within an ancient culture, we may not apply it directly today if the need is no longer evident. Rather, we look for parallel situations. When Jesus commanded his disciples to wash each other's feet, for example (Jn 13:14), he did so because they wore sandals and walked on dirty roads. We don't in North America; so we look for other practical needs to fill, even if the task is humiliating.

When a situation is culturally relative, only the underlying principle applies today. If, by contrast, an instruction has a rationale that is unchanging, then the instruction is universal for every time and place. If an instruction is grounded in God's character or order of creation or one of the Ten Commandments or the gospel of Jesus Christ, for example, there's no getting around it.

Is Paul's rationale against women pastors culturally conditioned?

Paul states his reason clearly: "For Adam was formed first, then Eve"

(1 Tim 2:12-13). Paul is arguing unambiguously from God's order of creation in Genesis 2:21-24. Adam's priority was established before the Fall and is part of God's good design.

Women and men are equal, but also different. And at least one office—the office of elder (or "presbyter," "overseer" or "pastor")—God reserves for a few, and those few, among the other requirements listed later in 1 Timothy 3:1-7, are to be men.

What is it about the way God has differently created men and women that makes leading the church best suited for men? It has something to do with God's design of the woman as the completion of another. It's not a question of spiritual gifts—we see the Holy Spirit fall upon both men and women, and both teach in the New Testament church. And it's not a question of one sex being better than another (Gal 3:28-29). Nor is it a question of ability—I've known very discerning, knowledgeable Christian women with tremendous public speaking abilities. Nor is it that women can never lead men—God raised up Deborah to lead Israel (Judg 4—5).

Rather, it seems simply to be a question of office—a particular office of authority within the church that God has designed with a man in mind. Whether or not I understand all the reasons, I trust God's judgment. And for two thousand years this has been the wisdom of the Christian churches.

Why This Rubs Us Wrong

Why is it that saying one office is designed with a man in mind so offends us? Why can't we just say, "Awesome! *Vive la différence!"?* The differences between the sexes are to be celebrated rather than denied. I think our American bias against authority is at the heart of the issue. The reason this rubs us the wrong way isn't a problem with the Scriptures but a problem with the readers.

We fail to understand the distinction between biblical categories like equality and authority. Biblically speaking, I can be under the authority of one who is my equal. Being under authority doesn't mean that we're "less important."

I've heard feminists—both outside and inside the church—say male headship can't coexist with equality of the sexes. Equality must mean interchangeability, they argue. Such thinking is incompatible with the religion of the Bible. Jesus was God in the flesh (Jn 1:14), coequal and coeternal with the Father, worthy of equal faith, glory, honor and obedience. Yet Jesus also submitted to the Father's authority, always doing what pleases the Father (Jn 8:29). He was "in very nature God," yet he "made himself nothing, / taking the very nature of a servant" (Phil 2:6-7). So was Jesus beneath the Father, or was he equal to the Father? *Yes, he was both.* If you can't grasp that notion, you'll understand nothing of the Bible's instruction about authority. You'll think Paul a sexist and government an evil institution. But according to God, equality and authority can go hand in hand.

Civil Government as a God-Given Authority

Just as God established marriage and structured it by vesting the authority to lead with the husband, so God established civil government. Theologians have debated when exactly God established government. We know that marriage was established before the Fall. I suspect government is likewise a good part of God's original design, with civil authority grounded in the mandate to subdue the earth and rule over it (Gen 1:28).

Had sin never entered the world, for example, authorities still might have been needed to build roads and establish standards for weights and measures. If so, government is a *creation ordinance:* an institution God established forever at creation. Christians have historically talked about our obligations to the state when discussing the fifth commandment to honor father and mother.

God has established various institutions to order human society, each with its own sphere of activity and mission, but each accountable to him. This *sphere sovereignty* is a foreign notion to many. In totalitarian nations every sphere of society is dominated by one controlling institution, usually the state, as in the former Soviet Union. In revolutionary Iran, though, a religious organization dominated every other sphere of life, just as the Roman Catholic Church sought to dominate medieval Europe.

In the United States, by contrast, the individual is seen as the basic unit of society. Institutions within society are the creations of autonomous people. Children can divorce their parents, churches are membership organizations, and the federal government exists by social contract. This radically individualistic perspective accepts no authorities except those the individual agrees to.

The biblical vision for society centers not on the individual or any single institution, however, but a sphere sovereignty in which many different institutions function within God's design. Gordon Spykman explains:

All men live within a network of divinely ordained life-relationships. People do not find meaning or purpose either in their own individuality or as part of some collectivistic whole. Rather, people fulfill their callings within a plurality of communal associations, such as family, school, and state. God ordained each of these spheres of activity as part of the original order. Together they constitute community life.[5]

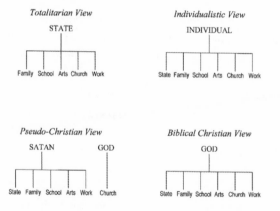

If every area of life has its origin in God, then government—like the other spheres—can't be arbitrary in its actions. The United States Congress receives its authority to rule from God—not just from the people— and is therefore accountable to God's law.

---

[5]Gordon Spykman, "The Principled Pluralist Position," in *God and Politics: Four Views on the Reformation of Civil Government,* ed. Gary Scott Smith (Phillipsburg, N.J.: Presbyterian & Reformed, 1989), p. 79.

According to God, Government Legislates Morality

Does this mean that the government can legislate morality? Of course. Every law on the books legislates morality. While driving to the gas station today, I wore my seatbelt. Why? Because the government makes me. Why would they do that? Because seatbelts save lives, and it's wrong to risk human life. Killing is immoral, even if I'm my own victim.

But what if the people of a particular nation aren't Christian? Appeal can be made to God's law written in creation—to natural law. Indeed, the parts of Scripture that we seek to enforce through the state are precisely these areas. The sixteenth-century Genevan reformer John Calvin made this point well:

> It is a fact that the law of God which we call the moral law is nothing else than a testimony of the natural law and of that conscience which God has engraved upon the minds of men. . . . Hence, this equity alone must be the goal and rule and limit of all laws.[6]

Government and rulers have been around longer than the Bible, since the very dawn of human history. Government is not a uniquely Christian thing; it's a human thing, a gift God has given to every society since Eden. Even pagan rulers are placed there by a sovereign God. The governing authority "is God's servant to do you good" (Rom 13:4). Peter concurs; governors are "sent by him to punish those who do wrong and to commend those who do right" (1 Pet 2:13-14).

Because God's natural law still exerts its restraining influence within society (by God's common grace), it is possible to have a wise governor who is not a follower of Christ. I don't have to look for a Christian testimony before voting. As a voter I'm less concerned with whether a candidate is saved and more concerned with whether he or she will govern in a manner that's righteous.

I could vote for a Mormon or a Muslim if they'll further a godly vision for the nation—a vision they may have received from nature if not from Scripture. Like Martin Luther, who saw Muslim Turkish armies approaching the

---

[6]John Calvin, *Institutes of the Christian Religion* 4.20.15, trans. John T. McNeill (Philadelphia: Westminster Press, 1960), p. 1504.

gates of Vienna, I'd prefer a wise Turk to a foolish Christian. Actually, my top choice would be a wise Christian, but that's not always an option. When it comes to civic and moral matters, we can cooperate with others outside of Christ, not as allies, but as what Francis Schaeffer called *cobelligerents*—those fighting against evils we too oppose.

God calls us to work to reform corrupt governmental structures, to bring them more in line with his will. We aren't cramming our religion down anyone's throat; we're just living by the same truth when we vote as we live by on Sundays. If we didn't, we'd be inconsistent at best and hypocrites at worst.

Yet the fact that much of the Bible's moral content is written in creation means that I can seek to persuade the state to act justly even before the individuals involved are all converted to Christ. When I argue on behalf of the unborn before a secular audience, for example, I don't argue that abortion should be banned because "the Bible says so" (though it does). What I argue is this: everyone knows it is wrong to kill the innocent (and few will disagree here). Indeed, it is the government's job to protect the innocent, even if their deaths would be extremely convenient for many people (and few disagree here—this is written on their hearts). Since science shows us that the fetus is a unique, living human being (and I have facts to back this up), then the government's job is to protect the unborn, even if inconvenient for many. I've made many prolifers with this simple argument.

This isn't evangelism, but evangelism isn't the government's job. This is citizenship under God. Can we restore the good society God designed for us in the beginning through merely political means? Absolutely not. But we can help restore some aspects. We are salt and light in the world through our deeds as well as our gospel (Mt 5:16).

Government's Priorities According to God

What priorities should we take into the voting booth? What vision does God give for the state? In Scripture we see certain limitations on government's power—like when God judged King Ahab's house for stealing from a citizen what was not rightfully the king's (1 Kings 21). And government is not lord of the conscience, so we see it regulating only actions, not thoughts. Similarly, we see government in this era primarily concerned with humanity's relationship with fellow humans. Our relationship with God is in the sphere of the church (Mt 28:18-20).

In Old Testament Israel, church and state were united in a theocracy, but church and state today are not united. By God's design, Caesar and God are separate (Mt 22:21). Still, within these limitations God gives government authority for several vital functions in preserving the society.[7]

1. God gives us government to punish criminals. The establishment of justice—giving to each his or her due—has been a function of government since the Fall. Scripture says punishment for the guilty must be done without favoritism toward rich or poor (Deut 1:17).

> *To show partiality in judging is not good:*
> *Whoever says to the guilty, "You are innocent"—*
>   *peoples will curse him and nations denounce him.*
> *But it will go well with those who convict the guilty,*
>   *and rich blessing will come upon them. (Prov 24:23-25)*

Christians don't like to talk about punishment. But God has a distinct purpose for the state, one that centers not on mercy but on justice. As we've already read, God established government to "punish those who do wrong and to commend those who do right" (1 Pet 2:13-14).

At least one crime has its punishment established for all people in Scripture: murder. While the individual Christian should forgive his or her enemy, and the church offers the guilty salvation through faith in Christ, the state's distinctive role in God's design centers on justice. In the case of murder, God tells us justice involves death.

Capital punishment—the most severe punishment the state can give—is grounded in God's covenant with Noah, which was a reestablishment of the creation order. After God destroyed all but Noah and his family, he reinstituted his covenant of creation but added certain stipulations to insure the survival of the human race. One was the

---

[7]I am indebted to David C. Jones at Covenant Theological Seminary, whose "Christian Ethics" course first helped flesh out for me the broad scope of God's calling on the state.

execution of those who shed human blood.

> *Whoever sheds the blood of man,*
>   *by man shall his blood be shed;*
> *for in the image of God*
>   *has God made man. (Gen 9:6)*

This isn't a prediction that every murderer is going to be murdered. Rather, it's a prescription, comparable to "You shall have no other gods." We know from Scripture that God relegates this tragic task to the state— private justice (vengeance) is prohibited in both Old and New Testament.

In such cases God requires us to send the guilty directly to him for judgment. This is why the National Association of Evangelicals, representing forty-two thousand congregations, fifty denominations and hundreds of parachurch ministries, has actively lobbied to assure a just but faithful use of this gravest of penalties. Consider these words from their 1972 convention:

> *The gravity of any crime is measured by the penalty it incurs. . . . If no crime is considered serious enough to warrant capital punishment, then the gravity of the most atrocious crime is diminished accordingly. . . . From the biblical perspective, if capital punishment is eliminated, the value of human life is reduced and the respect for life is correspondingly eroded.*

Yet God gives the state alone the authority to kill criminals—what Paul calls bearing the *power of the sword* (Rom 13:4). And God does not delight in the death of the wicked; therefore, neither should we. An execution is not a reason for celebration. But it is a job given to those God puts in civil authority.

God doesn't give us a list of specific punishments for other crimes as he did for ancient Israel. We do see some models, though. In addition to corporal and capital punishment, we see restitution—repayment for the wrong—as a part of the law code given to Israel (Ex 22:3).

2. God gives us government to insure equal opportunity and social justice. God gave Israel, for example, a year of Jubilee every fiftieth year. Slaves were freed, debts forgiven, and everybody received back their ancestral lands (Lev 25:8-55). God mandated fairness in commerce and protected the disabled from abuse (Lev 19:13-14). Even farmers were required not to harvest the edges of their fields so that the poor could work for their food by harvesting the edges themselves (Lev 19:9-10).

The Scriptures are filled with concern for the helpless. God "defends the cause of the fatherless and the widow, and loves the alien, giving him food and clothing" (Deut 10:18). Foreign workers, widowed women and orphans were the most vulnerable of people. God warned ancient Israel of violent judgment if they took advantage of widows and orphans (Ex 22:22-24). Prophets called down judgment upon businessmen who failed to pay workers (Jer 22:13), a violation of the Mosaic code (Deut 24:14-15). Scripture shows particular concern that the poor are not treated unjustly. Isaiah even cursed government leaders who used legislation to restrict the rights of the impoverished (Is 10:1-3).

3. God gives us government to protect public health and safety. The laws God gave Israel included requiring a wall around the roof of flat-roofed buildings so that people wouldn't fall off (Deut 22:8).The underlying concern is the protection of human life. God even wants government to be concerned with bodily waste, regulating "where you can go to relieve yourself" and how it's covered up (Deut 23:12-13). Modern environmental and sanitation laws have ancient biblical precedent. Consider even the legislation to preserve a species (Deut 22:6-7), or to protect domestic animals from being worked without proper nutrition (Deut 25:4).

4. God gives us government to provide for national defense. We see this concern as early as Genesis 14, where Abram and his army use force to rescue Lot from foreign kings. For his act of war Abram received blessing from God's priest Melchizedek. But Abram refused to continue involvement after he had accomplished his limited and righteous goals, presenting for us an early example of a limited defensive war. God warns against a militaristic spirit that glorifies war, forbidding David from building the temple because he was a man of war (1 Chron 22:8).

Nevertheless, there is no blanket call to pacifism in the Bible. Jesus praised the faith of a Roman centurion—a soldier from an occupying army (Luke 7:1-10). While the individual is always to forgive enemies, and the church to offer the gospel of Jesus Christ, the state's God-given job is to insure justice. In some tragic instances justice makes warfare unavoidable. God required Israel to go to war at times (Josh 1:1-6). Still, war in itself remains an evil—albeit occasionally necessary—in a world that rebels against God.

5. *God gives government our money to accomplish these purposes.* Jesus commands us to "give to Caesar what is Caesar's, and to God what is God's" (Mt 22:21). Paul commands, "If you owe taxes, pay taxes" (Rom 13:7). The gift of government comes with the obligation to support our government with our taxes. To cheat the Internal Revenue Service is to cheat God and deny him thanks for his protection through the state.

Christians are commanded to live altogether *for* their government rather than *against* it. "He who rebels against the authority is rebelling against what God has instituted" (Rom 13:2). We follow God's design by humbly respecting God's authorities, even as we seek to bring all of society—government included—more fully under God's kingship.

Questions for Discussion

1. In what sense are believers freed from God's law? In what sense is God's law still our authority?

2. In what ways do you see a spirit of lawlessness in our culture today? In what ways do you see it among Christians? In your own life?

3. Can you name the Ten Commandments? Look them up (Ex 20). How would each one apply in your own life right now? State the moral principle of each positively using your own words.

4. What is natural law? What significance does it have for seeing the world according to God's perspective?

5. God has vested authority in the husband as leader within the family. Why would it be wrong to assume that this means that women are inferior to men? What does the Bible say about the equality of men and women? What does it say about the differences between men and women? If married, how do you work out these authority questions in your own marriage? If not, how might this affect your relationships with married friends?

6. What is God's design for civil government? Where do you see government needing the most reform? Support your opinions with Scripture.

5

WHY THE *MONA LISA* IS GOING TO HEAVEN

Culture According to God

"God saw that it was good . . . and said to them,
' . . . fill the earth and subdue it.'"
GENESIS 1:25, 28

O ne of the first Bible passages I memorized when I became a Christian was the Great Commission (Mt 28:18-20). These were the Lord's final marching orders to his troops before ascending to heaven. King Jesus had promised that the Holy Spirit would give world-changing power to every Christian. So he instructed us to make disciples of every nation. He told us to go to people, baptize them in the name of the Trinity and teach them to obey everything the Lord commands. Here we get the big picture for the church. All the little things the church does are part of the one big mission to disciple the nations.

The First Great Commission—the Cultural Mandate
What few realize, though, is that there are two great commissions in the Bible. The more familiar is in Matthew 28. But an earlier great commission was given to all humanity. In the beginning God spoke to our first parents:

God blessed them and said to them, "Be fruitful and increase in number; fill

the earth and subdue it. Rule over the fish of the sea and the birds of the air
and over every living creature that moves on the ground." (Gen 1:27-28)

It's easy to miss the importance of these words. These are God's
instructions for the human race, his vision of life for us. At its heart it's a
call to establish human society upon the earth. The Lord designed us to
fill the earth and subdue it. We were created to rule creation, to make
our mark upon the land. We were created to create, designed to design.
This is the first great commission, the foundation for human civilization.
This is called the *cultural mandate.*

Dominion + Nature = Civilization

Western society has become so specialized that we miss the simple fact
that dominion and culture go hand in hand. We often think of nature in a
romantic sense as untouched forest. But right now as I type, I'm sitting
on forest—on a chair. It's one of those teacher's, old-fashioned wooden
chairs with castors. Such chairs ultimately come not from a factory but
from trees.

Two things are necessary for me to have my old-fashioned chair: trees
and human dominion (including human creativity). Man subdues the
earth to get the wood and then impresses upon the tree his creative
power as an image of God, yielding a gorgeous chair, even if it feels like
cement.

God's marching orders for humanity? Make chairs, construct houses,
plant orchards, dam rivers, harness electricity, extract pigments and fibers
and paint Mona Lisas, turn the silicon on the beach into microchips, turn
roots into potato chips.

Industrialization and the environmental crisis that accompanies it have
given us a negative image of dominion—one divorced from our God-
given calling. Dominion means more than filthy strip mines and smog.
Dominion doesn't mean rape and pillage. It does mean, however, that
God's world is incomplete without humanity in its proper place.

As discussed in the last chapter, God established certain institutions,
like government and family, to structure the social order. It's important to

realize, however, that culture itself was what God commanded us to create. Human society is not something neutral. God doesn't simply regulate human culture; he establishes it. He is the trunk from which the various branches of human civilization grow and spread.

To miss the reason God created us is to denigrate the lofty callings God gives most of us. No Christian should feel guilty for engaging in "secular" matters if that's what God's designed him for! The doctrine of creation is the great neglected doctrine of Christianity. Tons of Bible passages never show up in Bible memory systems. "Go, eat your food with gladness, and drink your wine with a joyful heart, for it is now that God favors what you do" (Eccles 9:7). I'd like to mount that one in my office.

Are such worldly pursuits as farming, architecture and retail a waste of time? God says no. And whatever we do by faith in this life will stand in the age to come—whether mopping floors or designing bridges. At the end of this age, when sin is eradicated and the nations walk by the light of God, the best of human culture will stand. Of God's city we are told, "The kings of the earth will bring their splendor into it" (Rev 21:24). I doubt Louis XIV will be there, but I have to think some Christians in his court might present to God the Versailles palace and gardens as an offering.

Picture the *Arc de Triomphe*, the *Mona Lisa,* Shakespeare's sonnets, the '57 Chevy, Baker furniture, the Taj Mahal—all the glories of human civilization, only purged of their sinful histories, mixed motives and negative byproducts. All of them will come into God's eternal city as offerings to the fountain of pure goodness, truth and beauty. "The glory and honor of the nations will be brought into it" (Rev 21:26).

Though Genesis 2 and Revelation 21—22 (history's beginning and end) are alike in almost every other respect, the Garden in the end will no longer be a garden but a great city, the centuries of dominion having finally been redeemed to establish civilization forever with God at its center. The cultural mandate, despite humanity's sin and rebellion, will be brought to fulfillment.

But Beware Babel
Still, Scripture is full of warnings about the misuse of culture. The call to

build human civilization has been co-opted throughout history by men and women (usually men) with giant egos seeking glory for themselves rather than God. When human society rises up against the God who established it, the culture becomes defiled by its idolatry.

We read in Genesis 11 of a tower built by men who wanted to make a name for themselves (Gen 11:4). Built sometime after the great flood (Gen 6—9), the tower of Babel became a symbol of human civilization erected for the glory of man rather than the glory of God. God responded with a preemptive strike, scattering humanity throughout the earth and confusing our language to limit our ability to cooperate with each other in our cultural rebellion against him.

While cultural development was ordained by God at creation, it's easily hijacked by sin. Remember Nebuchadnezzar's pride at the kingdom he had established. Walking on the rooftop of his palace, he asked, "Is this not the great Babylon I have built as the royal residence, by my mighty power and for the glory of my majesty?" (Dan 4:30). It took seven years of insanity before this king would raise his eyes toward heaven and acknowledge that the Most High is sovereign (Dan 4:28-37).

Sadly, arrogance is the common cold of the cultured. Jesus praised the Father for hiding the truth from the wise and learned of this world (Mt 11:25). Within the mystery of his eternal purpose God has chosen more of the "have-nots" of this world than the "haves." "Brothers, think of what you were when you were called. Not many of you were wise by human standards; not many were influential; not many were of noble birth," Paul writes. "But," he explains, "God chose the foolish things of this world to shame the wise" (1 Cor 1:26-27).

My own experience has been that highly educated, prosperous Christians—those of us who are most likely to appreciate the arts and high culture—are easily infected by the arrogance that accompanies the cultured. We find it too easy to look down on working-class believers for their rhinestone-studded praying-hands paperweights, as if the beauty of the arts was for our glory rather than for God's. There's no excuse for our pride and judgment. While God established civilization, he will not share his glory with another (Is 48:11).

God Wants You to Enjoy Creation

Warnings taken, though, there are a thousand cultural goodies here for our delight—so long as we receive them humbly and thankfully as gifts from God. We're physical creatures, and our physicality is a good thing— God said so. He formed us out of physical dirt (Gen 2:7). He said the material world was *good,* even *very good* (Gen 1:31). The flesh that Scripture warns us about refers not to our bodies but to our fallenness and is usually translated today as "sinful nature" (i.e., Gal 5:17).

I'm not quite sure why some Christians through the ages have believed physical pleasure is bad. Maybe they're just deeply aware of their tendency to misuse and become addicted to pleasure. We shouldn't let anything master us (1 Cor 6:12). But God gave us beauty and plea- sure. Pleasure is a good thing. Though it can be abused, the correction to misusing pleasure isn't to avoid it but to receive it with godly joy.

Jesus certainly wasn't decadent or excessive—he didn't even own a house during his ministry (Mt 8:20). But he enjoyed eating and drinking. His enemies accused him of drunkenness and gluttony (Mt 11:19). Con- sider how willingly Jesus turned water into wine for an entire party of people (Jn 2:1-11). Obviously, he didn't consider celebration a bad thing.

Despite the risk of abuse, Jesus entered into pleasure and allowed others to do the same. And biblical wine was real wine. It was often mixed with water, but you could still get drunk on it (Eph 5:18). That's why Scripture warns us to be cautious (Prov 20:1). The Bible explicitly says that God is the one who gives wine to drink (or not drink), just like he gives us bread:

> *He makes grass grow for the cattle,*
> *and plants for man to cultivate—*
> *bringing forth food from the earth:*
> *wine that gladdens the heart of man,*
> *oil to make his face shine,*
> *and bread that sustains his heart. (Ps 104:14-15)*

God's world goes far beyond the bare necessities. When a woman poured an entire bottle of costly perfume on Jesus' feet, for example, he saw it not as a waste but as a "beautiful thing" (Mk 14:3-9). Did you notice the aesthetic judgment? Jesus could have said it was an appropriate action or a moral deed. Instead, he thought it beautiful. By the way, there are about forty references to perfume in the Bible, almost all of them positive.

God gave us his good creation to be used for our enjoyment. Pleasures serve as pointers to God, who is good, true and beautiful. Another verse neglected by Christian plaque makers says, "A man can do nothing better than to eat and drink and find satisfaction in his work. This too, I see, is from the hand of God, for without him, who can eat or find enjoyment?" He even adds a recommendation. "So I commend then enjoyment of life, because nothing is better for a man under the sun than to eat and drink and be glad" (Eccles 2:24-25; 8:15).

The strongest biblical words about pleasure, however, come not from the author of Ecclesiastes but Christ's apostle Paul. We usually think of false teachers being those who loosen God's standard, but the worst teachers, Paul warns us, are those who tighten it, calling good things evil.

> *Such teachings come through hypocritical liars, whose consciences have been seared as with a hot iron. They forbid people to marry and order them to abstain from certain foods, which God created to be received with thanksgiving by those who believe and who know the truth. For everything God created is good, and nothing is to be rejected if it is received with thanksgiving, because it is consecrated by the word of God and prayer. (1 Tim 4:2-5)*

The teachers Paul condemns saw the physical world as an evil thing. Spiritual people, they said, were people who gave up certain foods, marriage and sex. In reality, though, this ascetic self-denial was not spiritual but demonic and heretical (1 Tim 4:1). To say that something God gives us is intrinsically evil is to malign the character of God.

Certainly there is a place for giving up one blessing in order to pursue another—through fasting, celibacy or financial sacrifice. I've known many Christians who've given up potentially lucrative careers in noble fields in order to enter Christian ministry. Paul himself gave up his right to marry in order to better serve God (1 Cor 9:5, 15). But Paul's reasoning wasn't that marriage was bad; instead, he was pursuing a different good.

Pleasure is central to our relationship with God. We aren't called simply to believe in God; we're called to delight in him. "Delight yourself in the LORD" (Ps 37:4). The Bible refers to delighting in God as much as to repenting. Our affections are central to living the life God has for us. And God delights in us. "The LORD delights in those who fear him, / who put their hope in his unfailing love" (Ps 147:11). Our delight in him is grounded in his delight in us.

I'm convinced that our failure to read all of Scripture carefully—and particularly the Old Testament—has impoverished Christians' spiritual lives. Salvation becomes merely getting to heaven, as if we were trying to escape the world God made for us. Salvation is much more comprehensive. First and foremost it is *reconciliation with God* (2 Cor 5:18-19).

Warfare once existed with God in every area of our lives. But salvation brings reconciliation in every area: art, drama, literature, science, education, engineering, retail, sleep, entertainment. Everything in life is reconciled to the Almighty under the lordship of Jesus Christ.

Indeed, it was Jesus who prayed that we would be in the world, though not of this world (Jn 17:16-18). Often we get this backward; we become worldly in our evangelical ghetto. We find ourselves of the world but not in it. That's exactly where we can't influence the world for Christ.

Human culture within God's design is intended to display the perfections of God's character to the entire universe. Can anyone see the sheer beauty of God's creation and not think our God is good? I'm not just talking about the Grand Canyon, the Swiss Alps and squirrels. I'm also talking about Beethoven's Ninth Symphony.

High Culture and the Arts According to God

Art is a sphere of life that has the potential to display God's beauty more than any other. Perhaps the term high culture is unhelpful. It conjures up images of snooty rich ladies in formal gowns. Still, the arts often display a culture's greatest accomplishments. Much of the world's truly great art displays the goodness of God, even though many of the artists have not been Christians.

I have no idea Beethoven's intention when he penned the Ninth. But his work still glorifies God. What comes through—willingly or unwillingly—is beauty that can be accounted for only by God's image in Beethoven. The ugliness of an artist's sin and the beauty of his music can be distinguished, and I can be thankful for the one even while I mourn the other.

Many great hymns are sung to tunes that were originally bar songs. The tunes were good! Even in the creativity of pagans God's goodness, truth and beauty are still on display since human beings are created in his image.

Even Paul quoted pagan Greek poets, including a *Hymn to Zeus* (Acts 17:28). Let's face it: the apostle was artsy. He had a thing for sixth-century B.C. Greek literature, the way he quotes it at opportune times to prove a point. He'd obviously spent some time reading the stuff—maybe it was his shtick. He cites the poet Epimenides as evidence that Cretans are all liars (Tit 1:12), and moral advice about bad company corrupting good character from a Greek comedy by Menander (1 Cor 15:33).

I personally prefer 1970s British science fiction over classical Greek literature. Still, *Doctor Who*—though definitely not a Christian show—has certain noble themes that I can appreciate: a love for peace, a recognition of human weakness and a sometimes dogmatic respect for the value of human life. Maybe if Paul were here, he'd watch a couple episodes with me.

Did you realize that the first ability actually called a gift of the Holy Spirit was art? Bezalel and Oholiab were given the Spirit of God to enable them to fashion the artwork in the tabernacle (Ex 31:1-11). God called Bezalel to work with wood and metals, while he gave other men gifts to weave garments. American men may not form after-church sewing circles, but God sees nothing effeminate or unspiritual about the arts.

God's perfection is the very standard of beauty. The one thing David longed for was to "gaze upon the beauty of the LORD" all his days (Ps 27:4). God is the unchanging standard of loveliness. Thus Scripture teaches us to think about whatever *is* lovely (Phil 4:8).

But while beauty may have an objective criterion in God's beauty, we as God's images have tremendous freedom to express that beauty creatively. Look at the sheer variety of art in the Bible: three-dimensional sculptures (Ex 25:18) and bas-relief carvings (2 Chron 3:7). Biblical art does not always have a religious subject. Solomon's throne was overlain with gold, inlaid with ivory with a rounded top, had two lions flanking the armrests and twelve more lions flanking the six steps (1 Kings 10:18-20). The decoration had no overtly religious content.

Christian music can include a love song to a wife, for example, not just love songs to Jesus. The Song of Songs is a prime example. Song of Songs is about a man and a woman in love with one another. Why is it in the Bible? Because God made men and women and bodies and love and marriage and sexuality, and the Holy Spirit chose to inspire a godly reflection on a relationship involving all of these.

It's okay for art to be secular. *Secular* doesn't mean "godless" but "temporal," taking place in this age, in time, from the Latin *saeculum,* meaning "a long time." After the Protestant Reformation when secular life was again recognized as a calling from God, we see the rise of secular themes in art. Indeed, we see it first in Calvinist Holland, where Rembrandt painted religious art like *The Return of the Prodigal Son* or *Three Crosses* as well as secular art like *Side of Beef Hanging in a Butcher's Shop* or *The Anatomy Lesson of Dr. Tulp.* Art need not have a religious subject to be Christian. All of life is given by God and is therefore worthy of contemplation.

Furthermore, art need not be functional to please God. Most of the adornment in the temple had no function other than decoration: pine paneling overlain with gold and decorated further with palm trees and chains, precious stones and gems, decorative beams and doorframes (2 Chron 3:4-7). Their function was beauty. Beauty is a noble end. And the blue pomegranates embroidered into the priestly robes (Ex 28:33) demonstrate that Christian art also need not be realistic; pomegranates don't naturally come in blue.

We also see dancing in the Scriptures (Ex 15:20), instrumental music with an array of instruments (Ps 150:3-5), a symphony with four thousand instruments and three parts (1 Chron 23:5-6), and even a little drama (Ezek 4:1-3). What strikes me is that no biblical author defends any of these artistic expressions. The authors assumed that the arts were worthy in God's sight.

Don't Be Crummy for Christ

There have been Christians who see ugliness as a mark of spirituality—what a friend of mine calls being "crummy for Christ." Maybe they've just overreacted to a materialistic culture, but they fail to realize both the goodness and the beauty of creation (Gen 1:31). When a church builds a beautiful building for worship, these are usually the first to criticize.

I'm not saying churches should blindly throw money into building projects. The tithe, for example, was designed for the Levites (the priests) in the Old Testament and should go to Christian pastors and missionaries today (Num 18:21). It would be a crime to rob Peter to pay Frank Lloyd Wright. But if believers want to sacrifice beyond that to build a building whose beauty draws their minds to God, more power to them. It can be a wonderful thing so long as the desire is to bring honor to God and not just outdo the church down the street.

Christ doesn't ask us to be crummy for him. God would rather receive no offering from us than an offering that lacks excellence (Mal 1:6-14). This biblical call for excellence should give us pause.

Some time ago I went to a local shopping mall to investigate the current state of Christian culture. I spent some time in a secular toy store and found some really neat things for less than two dollars: a miniature Etch A Sketch on a key chain, a top that flashed different colored lights when I'd spin it. They also sold candy.

Later I walked across the mall to a Christian retail store. The toys there were a lot more expensive. And frankly, they were tacky and used God's name in vain. I found a top there that cost more, didn't flash or anything, and said, "God is tops." My stomach was turning. Instead of Etch A Sketch key chains they had pencil sharpeners with the ubiquitous praying hands glued to them. They too sold candy—Christian breath mints,

Christian chocolate bars and Christian fortune cookies—and the candy cost a small fortune too. Is this what Christian culture is—a poorly made and more expensive clone of what the world is doing, but with God's name plastered all over it?

Of course, there are nobler goals than merely physical beauty. Inner beauty is the highest calling of God. Scripture calls us not to judge people by outward appearances or try to impress people with jewelry and wealth but instead to develop the inner beauty of a godly character (1 Pet 3:3-4). Sometimes the most beautiful things are the most simple, authentic and unadorned—like a godly character, a sincere act of love or a frank discussion with an open, honest person. Beauty in God's eyes is not limited to the flashy, the sophisticated or the expensive.

Our hearts should long to see God's beauty reflected in all we say and do, be it simple beauty or elaborate beauty. Of course, since we tend to see beauty as a means of exalting ourselves, we need to constantly check our attitudes for pride. The problem isn't with beauty, though, but with us.

There are times when all of us need to give up good things because they've become idols to us. In the wilderness, for example, God called the Israelites to look to a bronze snake for healing (Num 21:4-9), but the people soon began to worship the snake, and God called for it to be destroyed (2 Kings 18:4). The author of Hebrews tells us to throw off everything that hinders us—even the good things (Heb 12:1). Some Christians have to give up sports because it makes them angry. Others have to give up certain foods because they can't eat them responsibly. The Bible doesn't universally instruct us to abandon the good things of this world, but it does caution us to not become engrossed in them (1 Cor 7:31). If we delight in God's gifts more than in God himself, it may be time to give up one good thing in order to receive his gifts with a right heart.

We never judge *other* people for not giving up good things, though. That's the mark of a legalist. "For why should my freedom be judged by another man's conscience" (1 Cor 10:29)? Even Paul gave up certain God-given blessings such as the right to marry, to receive money for his ministry and sometimes the right to eat certain foods. He did so not because such things were bad but because he felt he could further the gospel better without them (1 Cor 9:4-5, 15, 27).

God doesn't stop with the basics, but "richly provides us with everything for our enjoyment" (1 Tim 6:17). He didn't have to create us with color vision or taste buds. That was a splurge on God's part. Indeed, heaven is pictured as a feast on more than one occasion (Lk 13:29). We need discernment in receiving pleasures because of problems with us, not with them. If received with the right attitude, even the most opulent of the world's cultural riches can be a source of personal delight and thanksgiving to God.

Culture, Dominion and the Environment

With all this talk of beauty in God's creation, How does the biblical vision of human culture, with its emphasis on dominion over nature, lead us to act toward the environment? Christianity has been attacked for fostering ecological irresponsibility—a charge I consider baseless. There is nothing wrong with the concept of dominion itself. Any action we take to heal the environment requires the exercise of human dominion over nature, be it breeding endangered species or removing pollutants from the sky.

Acting on the earth is not unnatural. When ants tear up the ground, tunneling under the soil and marring the landscape, we don't think there's anything wrong with the ants. They make anthills by nature! On one level, at least, human cities aren't all that different from anthills—humans build civilizations by nature, though as image bearers of God we bear a special responsibility for *how* we build.

It's our God-given calling to interact creatively with nature. Nature finds its completion when people live within it. The question isn't dominion or no dominion. The right question is how *ought* we exert our influence over nature.

First of all, we need to keep our dominion in biblical perspective. Though we have dominion, we remain creatures. We are not God. While we are over the creation with respect to nature, we are on the same level as nature with respect to God. We are fellow creatures, animated dust

(Ps 103:14). The covenant God established with Noah was not made merely with humanity. It was a solemn agreement between God and the birds, livestock and all the wild animals too (Gen 9:9-10). Our heavenly Father feeds the birds just like he feeds us (Mt 6:26). We are all derived and dependent creatures.

And remember that we were placed in the Garden with the directions "to work it and take care of it" (Gen 2:15). Our leadership of nature is a stewardship. We look after God's creation for him. The creatures are God's creatures (Ps 104:24), his works, in which he delights (Ps 104:31).

And the dominion God gives us is not self-regulated. We exercise it under God's law of love for him and neighbor. The command to love God includes within it the call to love what he loves—including his creation. Even the Mosaic legislation God gave Israel included protections for animals to prevent the extinction of species (Deut 22:6-7).

Similarly, God protected oxen from being muzzled while treading out grain (Deut 25:4). If we're going to use an ox to do our work, then we can't hinder the animal from eating while it works. While our dominion over animals—at least since the flood—includes the freedom to eat them (Gen 9:3), God forbids cruelty to them. Human sin is the real problem behind the ecological crisis of our day—particularly greed, the root of all evil (1 Tim 6:10).

Creation itself pleads with us to consider the noble calling God gave it. The animals, trees and even the atmosphere have the same final calling humanity does: to display the character of God. "The heavens declare the glory of God; / the skies proclaim the work of his hands" (Ps 19:1). If nature does that, then to damage nature is a pretty serious crime—a sin that God will judge: "The time has come . . . for destroying those who destroy the earth" (Rev 11:18). The Scriptures call *all* creatures to praise God's holy name (Ps 145:21), and God called the animals to increase and fill the earth as well (Gen 1:22). If each of the millions of species on earth has a calling from God to fulfill, then every species we exterminate diminishes the display of God's glory. Environmental concern is a *theological* priority.

God calls us to establish human civilization for his glory, not for our own. He also calls us to serve the rest of his creation by enabling it to glorify him as well. We cannot do one at the expense of the other. The cultural mandate gives us God's perspective on human society—civilization according to God. Certainly culture can be manipulated as a tool of godlessness. Nevertheless, the cultural mandate stands as a divine directive to every generation of people to establish human civilization on the earth and to do so for the display of God's goodness, truth and beauty.

Questions for Discussion

1. What was the first great commission? What did God call humanity to do?

2. What warnings does God give us to guide our cultural engagement? What biblical and historical examples do we have of the cultural mandate being hijacked for godless purposes?

3. What purpose do pleasures serve within God's world? List any pleasures today that God calls good but some believers may consider unclean.

4. Do you have any feelings about the current state of the arts in our culture? What about the current state of Christian involvement in the arts?

5. A friend wants to take on a part-time job to save up so she can decorate her home, but her husband won't let her because he says that real Christians don't waste money on frivolous things like that. They have plenty of money in the bank and give generously to their church and to missions. How would you help them think through the issues?

6. Are there any good things that you've had to give up because they became idols to you? Do you find it hard not to judge other Christians who seem able to receive that gift with thanksgiving?

7. What reasons do Christians have to care about the environment? Read Romans 8:19-22. What additional biblical reasons can you see?

6

KNOWING GOD, 9 TO 5

Work According to God

*"The LORD God took the man and
put him in the Garden of Eden to work it."*
GENESIS 2:15

I remember hearing a woman who was raised Catholic give her testimony. After listening to a Christian friend talk about how central God was in her life, she insisted, "Oh no. You're not going to get me into the convent, sister!" Only when her friend explained that following Christ didn't mean entering a convent was she willing to give the gospel a fair hearing.

Jesus Was a Second-Class Christian

Often in Christian spirituality serious believers have been those in the monastery, the convent, the pastorate or mission field. Ordinary Christians—laypeople—weren't as blessed as the folks doing Christianity full-time. Of the two types of Christians in this dualistic vision, only the former is really used by God to his or her fullest potential.

It's sad that a lot of sincere Christians have adopted this dualistic ethic: If you really love Jesus and follow his call, you'll become a missionary. Christians who are totally committed to God don't do secular work. They do work that has eternal significance, "Christian" work as pastors or missionaries.

For Jesus' first thirty years on earth he did carpentry. That's a secular job. And though men called him Rabbi during his last three years, he really wasn't one, strictly speaking. He was even ridiculed in his own hometown when he got up to read in the synagogue. "Isn't this the carpenter?" (Mk 6:3). The implication is clear: This guy works with his hands like the rest of us. What makes him so special? Come on! It's not like he's a priest!

Jesus could have spent more of those first thirty years preaching, but he didn't. Why not? Because God called him to spend thirty years doing carpentry, then God called him to spend three years preaching. Both callings honored God.

Preaching the gospel is important. Salvation doesn't come to people through nature—they'll believe only if we send them a preacher (Rom 10:9-15). But preaching wasn't God's original design for us.

Look back to the beginning to God's pattern for us. Before sin ever entered the world, what did Adam do? He worked. "The LORD God took the man and put him in the Garden of Eden to work it and take care of it" (Gen 2:15). Adam had a job. And we can't blame his job on sin. We were made for work.

We often fail to realize that the calling to work—whether a ministerial job or secular job or family chore—is one of the Ten Commandments. The fourth commandment not only reminds us to rest on the sabbath but also commands us to work six days a week. "Six days you shall labor and do all your work" (Ex 20:9). This doesn't mean working outside the home six days a week. It includes all work—housework, homework and office work—whatever is work to us. We are, by nature, *homo faber*, working man.

We miss part of our humanity when we do nothing. We were made to find fulfillment in our calling, whatever that might be. To use a little theological jargon, work is a creation ordinance, part of God's original pattern of life. We were designed for the pattern of working six days.

The inability to do productive work hurts us. The Soviets understood this. They used to punish political prisoners by making them dig a hole one day and fill it up the next, repeated day after day for months. It would psychologically crush the inmates. It's part of our nature to do productive work. No wonder unemployment can be so devastating. Besides the sense of rejection and insecurity about the future, there's a real sense that you're missing what you're made to be.

Not Just a Job but a Calling

In the last chapter we discussed God's first great commission for humanity, the cultural mandate (Gen 1:28). Every type of work that people do, if it furthers our human mission of cultural development, is not merely a job but a calling from God. All work—unless it involves open rebellion against God—can be God-honoring work.

A job as a civil engineer, then, is not a bad thing. It's not even a neutral thing. It is a holy and spiritual calling from God. It's a position of significance in accomplishing God's great purpose for the earth. To build up human culture, to strengthen the social order through holy means—there is no higher occupation within God's plan.

Our jobs aren't just jobs. Scripture refers to them as *callings*. Explaining to servants not to leave their masters without first gaining their freedom, Paul writes, "Brothers, each man, as responsible to God, should remain in the situation *God called him to*" (1 Cor 7:24, emphasis mine). This is the same term Paul uses for God's calling us to Christ (1 Cor 7:17, 20).

A normal, secular work life is a noble part of the Christian experience. "Make it your ambition to lead a quiet life, to mind your own business and to work with your hands, just as we told you, so that your daily life may win the respect of outsiders and so that you will not be dependent on anybody" (1 Thess 4:11-12). A quiet, respectable secular job with a livable wage is exactly what God wants for most believers.

When notoriously corrupt tax collectors came to Jesus faithfully seeking guidance, he didn't tell them to become missionaries. Rather, he instructed them to remain in their God-given callings in a Christian manner. "'Don't collect any more than you are required to,' he told them" (Lk 3:12-14). He did the same thing when Roman soldiers came to him. "'Don't extort money and don't accuse people falsely—be content with your pay'" (Lk 3:14).

So your pastor's job isn't more spiritual than the church janitor's. The difference isn't one of value. Positions that bear God-given authority are worthy of higher honor and respect from those under their authority. Thus Scripture instructs us, "Give everyone what you owe him . . . if respect, then respect; if honor, then honor" (Rom 13:7). I approach my pastor differently than my pastor's son. Still, both are equal, and both have jobs equally worthy before God. The difference is one of authority.

How to Discern God's Calling

We Christians tend to stress over discerning God's calling for our lives. It was probably a lot easier a few centuries ago. If your parents were farmers, you would be a farmer. Today the sheer number of options makes discernment more difficult. Lots of tests out there that can help people discern their vocation (literally, their *calling*), or at least get you started in the right direction.

Then there's the infamous question, "If you won a million dollars, what would you do?" If you'd build a racecar, you should probably investigate engineering. If you'd cook all day, then you should work as a chef. Unfortunately, a lot of us would just watch TV all day, which likely reflects our laziness, not our calling.

People often ask me why I left architecture to attend seminary and (eventually) teach theology. I loved architecture. I'd wanted to be an architect since first grade. But when I got to college, I found myself rushing through my architecture work just to read theology books. While gluing balsa wood together I was wishing I was preparing a Bible study for my small group. After prayerfully talking things through, it was clear that my calling wasn't architecture but vocational Christian ministry. So I went to seminary.

While at seminary I was able to compare myself to others with callings in Christian ministry and I started to see that I was called to teach theology—another piece of the puzzle. Next I needed a Ph.D. While pursuing doctoral work I could compare myself to other people called to teach theology, and it became clear to me that my real passion was to teach ordinary Christians theology.

People sometimes ask me what it felt like to receive a call into the ministry. The truth is, *it didn't feel like anything*. I didn't have any burning in my bosom or quiver in my liver. I just thought through what I was best designed to do. Other people helped me assess my strengths and weaknesses and weigh my options rationally. I prayed, not hoping to hear a voice, but to express to God my dependence on him to guide me.

I was never 100 percent sure of my calling. I just made the best decisions I could at each moment, and God kept me on track. If that sounds unspiritual, you probably need to study biblical guidance. I have never found a verse that says God leads us through emotional experiences.

God created our minds to image his rationality. He wants our decision-making to image him, which means we can't turn our minds off and expect the Holy Spirit to take over. God is sovereign over even the tiniest details of our lives; so we know he'll lead us even if he doesn't tell us where exactly we're going. Our responsibility is to trust in him and walk according to his counsel.

Imaging God on the Job

Whatever your calling, your work life is your primary opportunity to display God's image. Chapter three discussed five characteristics of God's image in us: knowledge, creativity, righteousness, dominion and community. Knowledge is a big one, becoming increasingly central to many professions as society becomes more specialized.

But even in jobs that aren't information-based, opportunities to image God intellectually abound. I used to work in a kitchen store, and we had to know our products to do our job well. So I learned about the conductivity of metals, the durability and nonstick properties of different coatings, and the difference between an ice-hardened forged blade and a stamped serrated one. Creativity also played a role—setting up displays, marketing items and even doing a little cooking.

And my job was certainly a call to image God's righteousness. Difficult customers provided opportunities for me to learn forgiveness and patience. The day I dropped the jar of barbecue sauce and it exploded on an immaculately dressed lady's white pants also gave me the opportunity to learn to accept forgiveness when I've done something really,

really bad. And there were really nice customers who could have been easily suckered. I could have manipulated people into buying more expensive products than they needed. For the most part I refrained, though there was a constant moral battle.

And our regional manager pressured us to sell nitrous oxide canisters—whipped cream chargers, also known as laughing gas—to children. You'd be shocked at the number of twelve-year-olds sent in by their moms to buy whipped cream chargers. It's legal to sell them to kids, though sniffing the drug can be harmful and potentially fatal. So I refused to sell them to minors, disobeying my boss in order to be faithful to God (Acts 4:19).

And I definitely was furthering human dominion over nature. I helped tons of people better exert dominion over cows and chickens—especially the barbecued kind. My little job may have been only one tiny cog in the giant machinery of civilization, but it was an important cog nonetheless, even without any special recognition or a livable wage.

But I think the central aspect of God's image that we should see in the business world is community. In today's cutthroat, profit-driven world, relationships are often expendable. A biblical vision for commerce, though, sees business centering on the development of mutually beneficial relationships between people.

I used to have newsletters printed up at a large copier, for example. No matter how hard I tried, this company would not develop a relationship with me. They were cheaper than most and could produce a better product than anyone else. But they botched almost every job, usually because of a failure to communicate. Eventually I left and found a small company that values a relationship with me. They know my name and know exactly what I want. When something isn't working right, they call and tell me my options. What do they get? A little work, a little money and a highly satisfied client who'll recommend them to anyone. The relationship is at the heart of a godly vision for business.

Adam Had the Perfect Job, but He Lost It

If we're working in our calling and keep our attitude centered on Christ, we should find some satisfaction in the work we do. Indeed, finding enjoyment from our work "is from the hand of God" (Eccles 2:24). But work isn't always fun. When Adam ate the forbidden fruit, God laid a curse on our work as punishment:

> *"Cursed is the ground because of you;*
> *through painful toil you will eat of it all the days of your life.*
> *It will produce thorns and thistles for you,*
> *and you will eat the plants of the field." (Gen 3:17-18)*

Work after the Fall takes on a bitter flavor. It remains a calling but becomes a calling filled with pain. Adam's job was to work the garden (Gen 2:15). He didn't have an expensive tractor to ride on. Thorns and thistles meant suffering on the job. Adam was given the perfect job, but he lost it. His new job looked a lot like the old one, but it felt a lot more discouraging. And, unfortunately, this aspect of the curse doesn't go away when you become a Christian.

Pain and frustration aren't the only effects of the Fall on work. Our attitudes are rarely content with what God has given us. Even if you work just eight hours a day, that's a third of your daily walk with God. It comes as no surprise then that so much of our struggle with sin can revolve around the workplace.

Our efforts to fight sins like criticism, factions, gossip, anger and complaining are likely to be played out on any job. And jobs in Christian ministry aren't completely different. We're all sinners, though you see more people asking each other for forgiveness when your coworkers are Christians. Sins like gossip and complaining crop up in all our relationships. There are three issues, though, that are dysfunctions of work: job-hopping, laziness and workaholism.

Freedom from Job-Hopping

There is no biblical prohibition on changing jobs, and I wouldn't want anyone in a new job to feel guilty reading this. But God seeks loyalty, faithfulness and commitment in us. Faithfulness, remember, is a fruit of the Holy Spirit (Gal 5:22). Commitment to an employer is needed in today's world, and so is commitment to one's employees. Business isn't only about profit; the biblical bottom line is following God's call. An employer who keeps his employees' callings in view is an employer who likely fosters commitment in his workers.

The big problem with job-hopping isn't that a job is changed but that a calling is being resisted. Excessive job-hopping is usually symptomatic of deeper issues like discontentment with the life God has given us (Phil 4:11-13). Constant job-hoppers are often church-hoppers and spouse-hoppers too. The same heart issues are at play. Employers know this and put a resumé that lists ten jobs in ten years at the bottom of the pile. The underlying discontentment reveals a failure either to understand or to trust the sovereign hand of God (Heb 13:5-6).

God sovereignly overrules the circumstances of our lives so that we can say that wherever we are right now, we are exactly where he has called us to be. God's hand even lies behind seemingly random acts. "The lot is cast into the lap, but its every decision is from the LORD" (Prov 16:33). "The LORD works out everything for his own ends" (Prov 16:4).

Accordingly, it's wise to remain in the profession you're in until you have good reasons to think God is calling you elsewhere. Paul lays this down as a general rule. "Each one should retain the place in life that the Lord assigned to him and to which God has called him" (1 Cor 7:17). Paul applies this principle to getting circumcised (don't if you aren't), as well as to employment. "Each one should remain in the situation which he was in when God called him" (1 Cor 7:20).

It's not that a believer can never leave a job. Paul tells slaves to stay put—unless they can gain their freedom. "Were you a slave when you were called? Don't let it trouble you—although if you can gain your freedom, do so" (1 Cor 7:21). Jesus of Nazareth left his job when God called him to his preaching and miracle-working ministry. A job change is to be expected when a Christian is experimenting to discover his calling, or when God specifically leads him to a different calling. Still, Scripture leans heavily toward staying put until God directs you elsewhere. "Brothers, each man, as responsible to God, should remain in the situation God called him to" (1 Cor 7:24).

Freedom from discontentment begins in trusting that God has called you to the very job that so frustrates you. Your final responsibility isn't to your boss or clients but to God. The Lord is always your true client as well as your ultimate boss. And since your calling takes center stage in your walk with God, all his grace is available while you're serving him in the workplace. We work by faith in the promises of God.

Freedom from Laziness

My experience with job-hoppers is that they are often hard workers. Their weakness is rather a failure to find contentment when things aren't new anymore. For those the Bible calls sluggards, however, the opposite is true. Their characteristic is a dread of work to the point of irrationality. Sloth is not the same as weariness—even Jesus became tired and weary (Jn 4:6). Jesus was not lazy.

Laziness receives sharp condemnation in the Scriptures. "The sluggard's craving will be the death of him, / because his hands refuse to work" (Prov 21:25). An unwillingness to work is a crime against creation itself, a rebellion against part of our humanness. In Jesus' parable of the talents, the servant who didn't use what he had to further his master's wealth is condemned as a "wicked, lazy servant" and is thrown "outside, into the darkness, where there will be weeping and gnashing of teeth" (Mt 25:26-30).

Scripture calls our attention to animals as examples of God-honoring diligence in our work.

> Go to the ant, you sluggard;
>   consider its ways and be wise.
> It has no commander,
>   no overseer or ruler,
> yet it stores its provisions in the summer
>   and gathers its food at harvest. (Prov 6:6-10)

An animal's instinct to work assures its survival. Such wisdom is engrained in the fabric of creation.

While God repeatedly calls us to help people who are poor because they're unable to work due to calamity or oppression—people like widows and orphans—Scripture also commands us *not* to feed people who are hungry because of their own laziness:

> *For even when we were among you, we gave you this rule: "If a man will not work, he shall not eat." (2 Thess 3:10)*

Often Christians look at this rule in disbelief. How could a God of love be so unloving? I think when we see the situation through God's holy and righteous eyes we can understand that sin is an act against ourselves as well as against God. Sometimes we sinners need to feel the results of our actions.

It's not my job to make people feel the results of their sin. But God doesn't want us to underwrite the cost of rebellion. I hate the way our society keeps an entire class of people destitute yet hopeless, with millions of urban poor never learning to work but remaining dependent on government handouts that don't adequately provide for them. But many lazy people aren't poor.

What's more interesting are the prosperous suburban professionals who squeak by doing precious little work. There's a whole art to looking busy, shuffling papers, pretending to be productive. "We hear that some among you are idle. They are not busy. They are busybodies. Such people we command and urge in the Lord Jesus Christ to settle down and earn the bread they eat" (2 Thess 3:11-12). God commands us to work, but he has also united us to Jesus, and in him we can change.

Understanding God's sovereignty over our situation and reminding ourselves that it's not a job but a calling goes a long way to overcome the attitudes behind laziness. The Bible says that hard work on the job is "doing the will of God" (Eph 6:6). If what I do has no ultimate significance, Why bother? But if God will be glorified before all the angels in heaven, then I can roll out of bed and get to work. Anything I give is worth it. A calling demands my excellence.

If even a humble job is a calling from God, then our work isn't just a worldly activity to get money but an act of worship and service to God. Scripture instructs us, "Whatever you do, work at it with all your heart, as

working for the Lord, not for men. . . . It is the Lord Christ you are serving" (Col 3:23-24). This means that you're not making a latte for the
angry lady with all the shopping bags. You're making a latte for God. So
steam the milk even if it's iced, and don't skimp on the syrup.

Freedom from Workaholism

A third dysfunction of work—alongside job-hopping and laziness—is
workaholism. Half of the fourth commandment is a call to work. The
other half, of course, commands rest. "Remember the Sabbath day by
keeping it holy. . . . On it you shall not do any work" (Ex 20:8). God
doesn't always give us a reason behind his laws, but he does here. "For
in six days the LORD made the heavens and the earth, the sea, and all that
is in them, but he rested on the seventh day. Therefore the LORD blessed
the Sabbath day and made it holy" (Ex 20:11). We work because God
worked, and we rest because God rested.

God himself is our "Sabbath-rest" (Heb 4:9), a rest we receive from
Jesus when we stop trying to impress God and collapse upon the cross
of Jesus. Indeed, to enter into a saving relationship with God, we have to
give up self-effort and self-righteousness and renounce the myth of the
self-made man (or woman). "However, to the man who does not work
but trusts God who justifies the wicked, his faith is credited as righteousness" (Rom 4:5). The heart that's always rushing, addicted to work, is a
heart anesthetizing itself against the grace of God.

Our hurried lifestyles are every bit as unbelieving as sloth. Remember
the account of Mary and Martha. Mary sat at Jesus' feet while Martha
rushed around getting things done. Jesus spoke to Martha and told her
"only one thing is needed" (Lk 10:38-42).

Hurried people do not meditate on Scripture; they set a time limit and
never really enter into contemplation at all. They don't stop to thank God
for blessings. Hurried people are more concerned with what they do
than with who they are. They play the world's game but never find satisfaction. These are all characteristics of unbelief.

Into this hurried, workaholic lifestyle, God speaks the sabbath. In the
New Testament the sabbath appears to have become the Lord's Day, the

first day of the week (Acts 20:7; 1 Cor 16:1-2; Rev 1:10). In college when I first started observing the Lord's Day, it wasn't just an added rule. It was a revolution! Sunday had been catch-up day—laundry and homework. I hated Sunday. When I trusted God and committed not to work on Sundays, it radically changed my outlook on life.

For one thing, I found I had a ton of time on my hands, where before I was always working. It's a law of sin that the work expands to fill the time unless you limit the time under authority from God. I counted my time more carefully, but I really think something miraculous happened. My work time became twice as productive, and Sunday became my favorite day—a day for Christian friends, worship and deep, satisfying relaxation. I've never been tempted to go back.

Rest is every bit as much a creation ordinance as work. An addicted workaholic may think, *I don't need a sabbath.* If so, they're better than Jesus. He rested every sabbath, worshiping God in the synagogues of Palestine (Lk 4:16). The perfect man—the God-man—made the sabbath a priority.

Rest can involve entertainment, though I think we need caution here. The Messiah's kingdom is pictured with images of entertainment as well as security (Is 11:8). "The streets will be filled with boys and girls playing there" (Zech 8:5). But a lot of what we call rest is anything but restful. Studies have shown that people are more anxious after watching television than before, for example. And I don't play computer games on the sabbath anymore. I get too wound up. While I don't set rules for anyone but myself, I guard the Lord's Day to make sure it's a day of rest that prepares me to give six days of work in the coming week.

What God Thinks About Money

When we think of work, we eventually think of money. But work isn't essentially about money. It's about imaging God and fulfilling his cultural mandate. The central biblical instruction about money is that none of it is ours. It all belongs to God. We're only stewards. "The earth is the LORD's, and everything in it" (Ps 24:1). All wealth and possessions that end up under our oversight should be used prayerfully for God's glory. If you have a car, it's not your car. It's God's. He's just letting you borrow it.

God has given several legitimate directions for us to send his money. The first is to send it back to him. Giving should never be done reluctantly or under compulsion, "for God loves a cheerful giver" (2 Cor 9:7).

Generosity, according to God, begins with the tithe. God instituted the tithe sometime before Abraham, who paid it to Melchizedek (Gen 14:18-20). The tithe is the first 10 percent of the money God lets you oversee— and the first 10 percent comes before taxes. If you aren't willing to give that much, you aren't trusting God for the other 90 percent. I remember hearing one famous pastor tell about a man who asked the pastor to pray for him. The man had started making a lot more money and said he couldn't afford to tithe anymore. The pastor prayed, "Father, I pray you'd lower this man's income back down to the level that he can trust you with."

God accused the Israelites of robbing him when they skimped on the tithe (Mal 3:8-12). The tithe went to the Levites (Lev 18:21). Today this would include Christian ministers and missionaries spreading the good news of Jesus Christ. Jesus affirmed the tithe, though warned against neglecting weightier issues like justice, mercy and faithfulness (Mt 23:23). The early Christians gave a proportional amount of their income to the church on Sundays (1 Cor 16:2).

Still, we miss the heart of the biblical vision for money if we focus on the technicalities of tithing. The tithe is a starting point. The thrust of God's instruction is to have a generous spirit. Trusting God is in control, we're free to live lives of radical generosity. Those who sow sparingly will reap sparingly, but he who sows generously will reap generously (2 Cor 9:6). Think of the early believers in Jerusalem who sold their land to provide food for all the converts in Jerusalem after being converted at Pentecost (Acts 4:32-37). This is another biblical direction to send God's money—toward people in need.

Other than giving to God, charity and basic sustenance, money can also be used for pleasure—to have fun (1 Tim 6:17). Wealth can be a true blessing and is an opportunity to honor God (Prov 3:9-10).

This wonderful gift of God can be a powerful instrument to further his kingdom on earth. The Scriptures give examples of rich believers. Joseph of Arimathea used his influence to secure Jesus' body from the Roman authorities after the crucifixion, prepared the body himself and gave up his own new tomb—an expensive endeavor (Mt 27:57-60). Several women supported Jesus during his earthly ministry out of their own means (Lk 8:2-3).

Considering that Americans are only about 4 percent of the world's population but control about half the world's wealth, most who buy this book are rich Christians to most of the world. Though a great blessing, this can be a dangerous position. If wealth ever competes with God for your allegiance, God invites you to get rid of it. When I look at how low the giving is in most churches today, I fear that American churches are filled with people trying to serve both God and money. But "no one can serve two masters" (Mt 6:24). Remember that the love of money is the root of all kinds of evil (1 Tim 6:10). All God's good gifts have the potential to become idols, and money is one of the most powerful of idols.

Both poverty and wealth have their temptations—we're more tempted to steal when we're hungry, for example (Prov 30:9). But God has the power to overcome all these dangers and protect our hearts. He can teach us contentment whether we're in need or plenty (Phil 4:12-13). Surely the writer of Proverbs expressed wisdom when he wrote:

> *Give me neither poverty nor riches,*
> *but give me only my daily bread.*
> *Otherwise, I may have too much and disown you*
> *and say, "Who is the LORD?"*
> *Or I may become poor and steal,*
> *and so dishonor the name of my God. (Prov 30:8-9)*

Questions for Discussion

1. What are the major problems with the notion that secular work is less honoring to God than ministry jobs?

2. Read Genesis 2:15. What significance does this verse have on your life? Why is it so important that the passage is found before the Fall in Genesis 3?

3. What's the difference between thinking of your work as a job and thinking of it as a calling?

4. A friend doesn't know what God wants him to do with his life. How could you help him discern God's calling?

5. List the five aspects of God's image reflected in our work. How is each of these God-like qualities reflected in the work you do during the week?

6. This chapter discussed three dysfunctions of work: job-hopping, laziness and workaholism. Which most characterizes you? How does each deviate from the pattern God gave at creation and maintains throughout the Bible? What issues may lie behind each problem? How can a biblical understanding help a person trapped in each of these patterns?

7. What picture does Scripture give us of wealth and money? List as many facets of the biblical picture as you can. What is the one central biblical teaching about wealth?

8. Why do you think some Christians find it hard to tithe? Discuss whether this is the ultimate problem or is symptomatic of a bigger issue. What kinds of issues may lie beneath the surface? What kinds of things can you do to develop a generous spirit?

7

SCIENCE VS. RELIGION?

Science & Education
According to God

*"Whatever the man called each
living creature, that was its name."*
GENESIS 2:19

C hristian historian Mark Noll has criticized believers for failing to engage adequately with the sciences. We haven't been known for our thinking, he argues. "The scandal of the evangelical mind is that there is not much of an evangelical mind."[1]

While others have tempered Noll's cynicism, Scripture still leaves no excuse for mindless anti-intellectualism.[2] The pursuit of truth is central to Christian religion. Christian growth centers on the renewing of our minds (Rom 12:1-2), and Jesus commands us to love God with all our minds (Mt 22:37).

While many philosophies and religions have fostered science and

---

[1]Mark Noll, *The Scandal of the Evangelical Mind* (Grand Rapids, Mich.: Eerdmans, 1994), p. 3.
[2]Alister McGrath is much more optimistic about evangelicalism's future, suggesting that the movement is in its adolescence and shouldn't be expected to have funded a major research university—one of Noll's chief complaints. See Alister McGrath, *Evangelicalism and the Future of Christianity* (Downers Grove, Ill.: InterVarsity Press, 1995).

education, I'm convinced that the scientific revolution could never have taken place within a Gnostic religious context, for example. Why study the world if it's evil? Nor in Hindu India, where there's uncertainty over whether our world is real or an illusion. Christianity's insistence that God's world is both real and good (Gen 1:31) was the necessary foundation for the rise of modern science.

God's Two Books

The classic Christian expression about knowledge is the conviction that God has spoken to us in two books: creation and Scripture. These two books, nature and the Bible, are respectively *creational* and *redemptive* communication from God. Creation tells us what the world is supposed to be—it sets the pattern for life in this world. Scripture, by contrast, works to bring that ideal back into reality. But though creational and scriptural revelation have different functions, both "books" are truth from God. Consider the words of the psalmist:

The heavens declare the glory of God;
  the skies proclaim the work of his hands.
Day after day they pour forth speech;
  night after night they display knowledge.
There is no speech or language
  where their voice is not heard.
Their voice goes out into all the earth,
  their words to the ends of the world. (Ps 19:1-4)

God's glory in his works is displayed no matter what language one speaks. Seven times the psalmist states the same basic fact that nature has a message about its maker.

The psalmist tells us that the sky is speaking to us. Ultimately, of course, God is behind the picture. Nature doesn't speak all by itself—it speaks by the design of the one who made it to speak. God is whispering—sometimes actually roaring—through the cosmos. God is not the universe, but his glory permeates all he has made. His perfections shine forth in the order, design, beauty and changes of nature.

Granted, studying how chickens breed doesn't tell us anything about the cross of Jesus Christ. The message of the created realm is about the greatness, wisdom, power and beauty of God—not the history of redemption. Were nature enough for us sinners to have spiritual life, then God would have never had to enter history or choose Abraham or give him and his descendents the covenant. Nor would he have sent his Son to save the lost, engraft the Gentiles into Abraham's covenant or pour out the Spirit upon the nations.

Paul explains this dynamic in the opening chapter of Romans. "God's invisible qualities—his eternal power and divine nature—have been clearly seen, being understood from what has been made." But, Paul continues, the net result of this knowledge is "that men are without excuse" (Rom 1:20). Creation undeniably reveals God as creator. But when we're not holy, knowing there's a holy God does nothing to change our hearts or renew the divine image in us. Creation doesn't reveal God as redeemer, and we can have no God-honoring understanding of him without the salvation he's worked out in history and revealed in his Scriptures.

This is a huge qualification, but it doesn't change the fact that God's hand can be seen in the world he's created. The sciences have a theological significance because their object of study is the work of God himself.

Yet when we study God's world, we aren't just studying what God *did* ages ago at creation, we're hearing him speak to us *right now*. God is sovereign, and the universe continues to pulse with life by his sustaining power, not its own. To study the workings of the cosmos is to study the one making it work moment by moment. When you investigate how birds feed themselves, to use Jesus' example, you're really investigating how God is feeding the birds (Mt 6:26). When you examine the genetics behind the colors of lilies, you're really examining how God is dressing each flower (Mt 6:28-29). Science, like theology, is the study of what God is doing in creation. The seventeenth-century astronomer Johannes Kepler cried out, "O God, I am thinking thy thoughts after thee!"

The Divine Institution of the Sciences

The cultural mandate in Genesis 1:28 was part of the dominion God gave us. God also set up the sabbath rhythm of six days and one, placing his imprint upon time itself (Gen 2:2-3), and introduced work as an integral part of his design (Gen 2:15). Then we read a curious passage about naming animals.

Now the LORD God had formed out of the ground all the beasts of the field and all the birds of the air. He brought them to the man to see what he would name them; and whatever the man called each living creature, that was its name. So the man gave names to all the livestock, the birds of the air and all the beasts of the field. (Gen 2:19-20)

Here God calls Adam to categorize the creatures, a task that reflects our dominion. We name the animals; animals don't name us. But this passage isn't here just to let us know why chickens are called chickens. This is a call to learn from the created world, to understand it. God's call to name the animals functions as God's sovereign institution of science and education.

While God establishes some of the most basic categories for human understanding, he also calls us to develop categories of our own. This educational enterprise—learning about the world God gives us—finds its origin in God himself.

The fact that the sciences are derived from God means they're dependent upon him for understanding. Science finds its surest path when it embraces both God's books together. While I think Mark Noll's concern that Christian schools not neglect truth learned in creation is valid, the opposite mistake is just as bad. There's been increasing cultural pressure within Christian colleges to hire new faculty from top universities, even if their biblical and theological grounding is weak. God's two sources of truth do not function independent of each other.

We look at the world—God's book of nature—through the basic categories given us by God in Scripture. Creation isn't self-interpreting. As we'll see when we discuss Darwinism, the categories with which we interpret the world aren't always value neutral. If we assume that both God's books are true, then our goal is not simply to pull information from two sources—nature and the Bible—but to integrate these two sources of knowledge to see the world according to God.

When studying God's world we need the biblical foundation from which to discern the false assumptions that may underlie some research. If we fail to think Christianly about the world we live in, we find ourselves thinking in decidedly non-Christian ways, misunderstanding and misinterpreting God's world.

When Science Becomes a Monster

And our study of the natural world depends on God not only for our basic worldview but also for moral guidance. Like all of us, scientists work under the law of God—God's law revealed first in creation, then in Scripture. When independent of the God who gives it, science can become a monster.

I think particularly of the Nazi experiments on living human subjects during the 1940s. I'm also reminded of research today on aborted fetuses. It's an abomination before God to take a human life and then seek to profit from that evil through scientific advancement. No new knowledge is worth turning against God. People *always* take precedence over information gathering. The calling to science is a calling from God, but a calling subservient to the higher call to love God and neighbor (Mt 22:37-40). We're called to uphold his creation order.

Genetic engineering will raise new moral issues in the coming decades. Assuming human dominion over nature, I don't think Scripture prohibits every circumstance of altering genetic coding, but such research can only be honorable when constrained by love for humanity, care in stewarding creation and a firm respect for the integrity of each species as providentially given by God.

When researchers intermingle different species, they risk damaging the integrity of each species. Might some genetic material in other species prove helpful in preventing disease in humans? Perhaps. And God calls us to work against the effects of the Fall in every sphere of life. Yet science is also humbly called to learn from God's world, not to play God with his creatures. Science remains derived and dependent upon the Lord and finds its true significance only as it heeds God's law of love.

But notice that I'm not saying the sciences are under the church. The sciences are under God's law because all of human civilization is under God's law. But the sciences and the church are two different spheres. God established the sciences at creation with a mission to promote learning and knowledge. He established the church to redeem the world from its corruption with sin. Church and academy are separate, but both are derived and dependent on the Giver of the books.

We see the close interrelation between God's books in Psalm 19. After meditating on God's communication in nature, the psalmist contemplates God's law in Scripture.

> *The law of the LORD is perfect,*
>   *reviving the soul.*
> *The statutes of the LORD are trustworthy,*
>   *making wise the simple. (Ps 19:7)*

It's a natural progression for the psalmist from creation to holy writ—both have the same author and their messages complement one another.

We should beware of those who set God's books against each other—whether within the sciences or the church. God sees no conflict between his two lovely volumes. So when we look at the conflict between the biblical creation account and the evolutionary view reigning within the Western scientific establishment, we should see red flags.

Darwin's Challenge

In 1859 Charles Darwin published his book *On the Origin of Species by Natural Selection* and introduced the theory of evolution: the gradual development of all life from single-celled organisms. Darwin's agenda was as religious as it was scientific. His objective was to provide a scientifically believable theory to explain human existence without resorting to God or miracles. In this sense Darwin was a product of the Enlightenment, that great eighteenth-century secularization of knowledge. And what modernity demanded—a secular explanation of life—the Englishman Darwin willingly provided.

Evolutionary models infiltrated nearly every area of scholarship as well. With the broader rise of historicism in the modern era, historians and other scholars sought simply to trace the evolution of their subjects. Historians began to ask how events evolved, where events came from and where they were going. But it was no longer fashionable to ask truly important questions like *Was this good?* and *Was it right?*

Similarly, the arts and literature became characterized less by the pursuit of goodness, truth and beauty, and instead became about being avant-garde, progressive or ahead of the times—as if societal changes were of necessity good changes that made being ahead of them favorable! Even in my own architectural training, I remember studying the huge nineteenth-century change of mindset. Before that time architecture was about building beautiful and functional buildings using available technology. But in the nineteenth century, the question was no longer whether or not a building was a *good* building but whether it was a stylish building.

Hence the never-ending succession of styles that enable us to date a building in a glance. "Oh, a mansard roof. Second Empire. 1870s." "Ooh, round turret. Queen Anne. 1890s." "Streamlined terra cotta. Art Deco. Late 1920s." "Unadorned glass box. Modernism. 1960s." You get the picture. Whatever made us more concerned about being new than about being good? It's the secularized myth of progress working its way through every sphere of human knowledge.

In politics Darwinian thought forms also took advantage of the myth of progress. Liberal politicians want to move *forward* (whatever that means), while reactionaries are bad because they want to move *backwards* (whatever that means). Change is assumed to be good. The question people have been taught to ask is no longer *Is this right?* but *Is this the direction things are heading?* Again, such thought forms assume human events have a natural direction apart from any agency.

Even in theology, evolutionary categories made an impact. Scholars stopped asking what a book like the Gospel of Luke actually taught and instead started proposing how it evolved. I have no objection per se to the possibility of sources—Luke tells us others had written about Jesus (Lk 1:1). But who would have imagined that biblical studies, as taught in most universities over the past century, would have limited itself to such a narrow and more or less irrelevant area of study about which we can know next to nothing? All the while the actual theological content discussed in the biblical books is seriously neglected. The assumption that evolutionary processes can account for everything—and that those are the *real* focus of *academic* study—drove the academic fads that made so much twentieth-century scholarship worthless.

Darwinism is not a strictly scientific undertaking. Darwinism is inseparably enmeshed with nineteenth- and twentieth-century assumptions about progress, significance and goodness. Evolutionary thought carries with it certain moral and metaphysical assumptions. Such science is not neutral.

Four Unanswered Questions for Darwin

Still, for Christians who believe God has spoken truth in two books—books we dare not set against each other—there's an apparent conflict between what the sciences say and what the Bible says.

I think it's possible that we Christians have been misreading the Bible in some places, but we'll discuss this possibility later. First, let's consider whether the Darwinian establishment might be misreading God's book of nature. There are four questions that have yet to receive a satisfying answer from the evolutionary establishment.

1. How does life come from nonlife? The biggest problem with evolutionary science lies in evolution's very first step. The probability of even one of the simplest single-celled organisms developing from nonliving matter has been calculated at one chance in $10^{40,000}$.[3] That's a one with 40,000 zeros after it. I have no clue how they got this number, but the chances are effectively zero. For reference, the mathematical definition of impossibility is 1 in 10^{50}. Nonliving matter simply could not have turned into a living being—even a simple living being—no matter how spicy the primordial soup was.

---

[3]This is the conclusion of Sir Fred Hoyle, an agnostic and evolutionist. See Alan Hayward, *Creation and Evolution: Rethinking the Evidence from Science and the Bible* (Minneapolis: Bethany House, 1995), pp. 34-36 for discussion.

2. Are mutants really progress? Mainstream Darwinism proposes that variations between species result from natural selection whereby small mutations in the parent species over time add up to major differences— like birds from reptiles. The problem lies in the extreme limitations we observe on the positive effects of mutations. Mutations of any significance almost always end in sterile and weak animals that die off.

For natural selection to work, each tiny change in the evolutionary process would have to produce a positive benefit that helps it win out in the struggle to survive. The appearance of an eyeball, for example, would have had to include hundreds of individual mutations over time, gradually evolving into a complete eye. But what good is 5 percent of an eye? It doesn't give you even 5 percent vision. Such mutations would be limitations.

I was fascinated recently to read about one of God's tiny creatures, the ant lion.[4] Mr. Ant Lion lives in desert areas where preserving body moisture is essential for survival. He makes an interesting test case for the plausibility of gradual evolution. All of Mr. Ant Lion's systems appear to have been designed to insure his continued existence within his environment. His skin isn't water permeable (like nylon) and his mouth is clamped shut, both factors that prevent the loss of body moisture.

So how does the poor creature eat? He has a big straw sticking out of his face. When he catches his dinner, he makes two injections into his prey. The first injection paralyzes the victim; the second liquefies its innards. Mr. Ant Lion then inserts his straw and drinks a warm ant shake. And did I mention that Mr. Ant Lion doesn't urinate? (It's a delicate matter, I know.) His urinary tract dead-ends in a tiny sewage treatment plant that recycles the fluid back into his system, just like in science fiction novels.

What's important to realize is that none of the mutations are valuable unless all of them appear together. Not urinating would do no good if the

---

[4] French zoologist Pierre-Paul Grassé discusses the ant lion in arguing that traditional Darwinism fails to provide a mechanism for evolutionary change. Again, see the discussion in Hayward, *Creation,* pp. 24-28.

sewage treatment plant weren't in place. Drinking his prey like a milk-shake would be of no use if his skin were water permeable. The ability to drink his prey is useless without the equipment to liquefy his prey, and that's useless if he can't paralyze his victim first. No ant will hold still long enough to be liquefied, not even an exceptionally dumb ant.

Living organisms—even little guys like the ant lion—are complex and interdependent systems. If one part of the system is missing, the creature dies. This is a whopper of a problem with classical Darwinian evolution.

3. *Doesn't biological complexity trump appearance-based claims?* In college I wrote an article in a student newspaper questioning the scientific support for Darwinian evolution. The article was well received over all, but after several days the paper published a response article that proposed *comparative morphology* as proof of evolution.

I had never heard of comparative morphology and I was rather intimidated by this expert. So I asked some people who explained that comparative morphology is a fancy term meaning "comparing the shapes." Look at a photo of a chimpanzee fetus in the womb, then a human fetus. They look sort of alike. That's comparative morphology. I was underwhelmed.

Of course we look a lot alike. That doesn't prove causality. It could just mean that the same Creator created us. Look at Shakespeare's plays. *King Lear* and *Hamlet* look sort of alike. But that similarity doesn't prove that *Hamlet* evolved on its own from *King Lear.* It just means the same writer created them both. Demonstrating that a similarity exists does not demonstrate *how* that similarity came to exist.

This kind of argument was probably more impressive before the molecular revolution of the 1960s. We can now examine the chimp's and the baby's DNA and see lots of differences. Sure, some will add, there's almost a 98 percent genetic similarity between humans and chimps—but even 1 percent is huge! That's eighty million different nucleotides, give or take. Humans share most of their DNA with corn too—and nobody is arguing we evolved from corn.

Even at the biochemical level the various mutations within Darwin's proposal would each have had to result in a working and balanced system. To alter even the tiniest part of any of these systems results in failure of the entire system and the organism's death. Such a degree of evolution goes far beyond the natural limits of biological change.

No one denies the reality of *microevolution*—change below the species level. Different races of people have developed in different ways, for example. But people are all still people; our differences are minor. If my head is gushing blood, it doesn't really matter whether the blood they pump into me came from a Tibetan monk, a Scandinavian logger or a Tutsi tribesman so long as it's the right blood type. We share the same system; so our parts are fairly interchangeable.

By contrast, *macroevolution*—change that breaks the species barrier—though perhaps possible with the simplest of organisms, requires far too much impossibility to account for the development of the millions of radically diverse species on planet earth. Each species has an irreducible complexity that prohibits change at the species level or higher.[5]

4. *Where's the hard evidence in the fossil record?* For a scientific hypothesis to rise to the level of accepted truth, it requires hard data. The only hard evidence to test Darwin's thesis is the fossil record—the only record of what actually happened with life on planet earth. Charles Darwin and the early evolutionists predicted that thousands of transitional forms would be found.

Transitional forms are intermediate steps, missing links, between different species. There would theoretically be hundreds of forms just between modern man and our closest primate relatives. Darwin himself warned that without transitional forms in the fossil record, the theory of evolution was useless conjecture. Transitional forms either make or break his hypothesis.

A century and a half after Darwin *not one* incontrovertible transitional form has been discovered. Instead of thousands of gradual changes in species over time, the fossil record shows the different types of animals appearing abruptly, and then continuing with only minor adaptations until becoming extinct.

---

[5]See Michael J. Behe, *Darwin's Black Box: The Biochemical Challenge to Evolution* (New York: Free Press, 1996).

Generally speaking, the scientific establishment in the United States has been only grudgingly willing to admit weaknesses in classic Darwinism. As the issue has become politicized, revolving around control of public school curriculum, lines have become hardened.

A growing number of scientists, however, are admitting the lack of supporting data for classical Darwinism, among them Stephen Jay Gould, though not a creationist, who admits the lack of fossil evidence; Colin Patterson, a leader in his field; and Solly Zuckerman, engaged in ongoing debate with the anthropological establishment. Zuckerman has argued that there is no evidence for human evolution in the fossil record, and modern anthropologists rely far too heavily on guesswork and preconceived notions. He accepts evolution, not because of evidence, but because he self-consciously rules out the only alternative—creation.[6] Many of Darwinism's loudest critics are not creationists. They simply recognize Darwinism as a theory whose only evidence after one hundred fifty years remains circumstantial.

The lack of hard evidence for Darwinism has led Gould and others to develop the theory of punctuated equilibrium. Punctuated equilibrium suggests that species do exist in a condition of stasis. Evolution takes place in spurts so rapid as to leave no evidence. This enables evolutionary science to continue without empirical verification. More flamboyant proponents have even suggested that one species lays an egg and a radically different species hatches—the hopeful monster theory—so missing links would not appear between species.[7] But punctuated equilibrium cannot verify itself—it is an argument from silence.

---

[6]See Solly Zuckerman, *Beyond the Ivory Tower: The Frontiers of Public and Private Science* (London: Weidenfeld & Nicolson, 1970). Phillip Johnson provides a helpful discussion of Zuckerman in *Darwin on Trial* (Downers Grove, Ill.: InterVarsity Press, 1991), pp. 83-85, 192-94.

[7]University of California-Berkeley's Richard Goldschmidt argued for his "hopeful monster" by demonstrating specific changes that could never have arisen out of accumulated minor mutations. Darwinism provides no mechanism for changes beyond variations within the species level, he argued, so evolution must have taken place in rapid leaps rather than in gradual development. His theory, though repudiated by the Darwinian establishment, has been rehabilitated in part by Stephen Jay Gould.

Three Christian Perspectives

Since the mid-1980s the Intelligent Design movement has focused on identifying scientifically demonstrable evidence for design in nature.[8] Their focus has been on substantiating the fact of design, regardless of how that design was carried out. They critique Darwinism strictly on philosophical, methodological and scientific grounds, stressing particularly Darwinism's naturalistic assumptions.

The strength of the Intelligent Design movement has been in its reliance strictly on scientific argumentation, without appeal to the Christian Scriptures. The movement helps establish belief in a cosmic Designer— whoever or whatever that Designer may be—as a scientifically credible option within academia.

Christians, however, have more than just scientific data. While the Bible isn't a biology text and doesn't answer every question we put to it, we acknowledge the Scriptures as inspired and trustworthy in all they affirm, whether matters of history or religion. In contrast to the reigning view of origins within the modern scientific establishment, the Scriptures give us an account in Genesis 1—2 of God fashioning a first human out of inanimate earth, breathing into him and giving him life. The conflict is apparent, and we owe believers a response to the immediate question: *How does what we learn from science fit with what the Bible says?*

Despite numerous variations, Christians have taken three primary approaches to resolving this apparent discrepancy.

Theistic evolution. Before I became a Christian, I assumed that evolution was a scientifically proven fact. American public education, whatever the reason, insured that I only saw evidence for Darwin's theory.

So when I became a Christian, I still assumed evolution, but now understood that God oversaw the process. I held to theistic evolution— evolution under God's direction. For me, this was a transitional viewpoint, but a few truly great Christian theologians have argued in its favor—B. B. Warfield among them. Theistic evolution is a sincere attempt

---

[8]Leading figures in the Intelligent Design movement include Michael Behe, Walter Bradley, Michael Denton, Phillip Johnson, Dean Kenyon and Charles Thaxton.

to reconcile truth from Scripture with truth from the sciences.

But theistic evolutionists often consider the biblical account of Adam and Eve little more than myth, which poses serious questions. Genesis presents an unbroken historical account from Adam in Genesis 2:4 through Joseph in chapter 50. Linguistically, there is no genre change to justify declaring Genesis 2 as mythical. The New Testament certainly views the opening chapters of Genesis as historical, consistently regarding Adam and Eve as real historical figures, pointing out that Jesus descended from Adam (Lk 3:38).

The chief biblical text that—I am convinced—rules out theistic evolution is Genesis 2:7, where Adam becomes a living soul. Theistic evolutionists suggest that God created the first humans by breathing a soul into a highly developed primate. But its easy to miss a parallel here. The animals, the passage tells us, had already become living souls (*nephesh chayah*) in Genesis 1:20 and 1:24. The fact that the text states Adam "became" a *nephesh chayah* (Gen 2:7) implies that he wasn't already one. He was not formed from an existing primate but first became a living creature when he became a human creature.

To many this seems very technical. But it's important for us to realize that God has given us a historical narrative of the event. Our Lord has spoken with precision, so we must listen to his words with precision.

Young-earth creationism (creation science). The authors who helped me understand the weakness of evolutionary science generally coupled their creationism with a belief that the universe is very young—perhaps only six to ten thousand years old.

Creation scientists argue that God made the universe with the appearance of great age. The fossil record is understood to have been lain down by the Noahic flood, and these authors point out instances in which the strata at which fossils are found occasionally conflict with the standard dating. Proponents challenge the reliability of radiometric dating and at times suggest that the laws of physics have changed since creation.[9]

I value the firm commitment to Scripture these men have displayed

---

[9]The principal architects of this apologetic approach are Henry Morris and John Whit-

and the wonderful conviction that, were science done properly, it would agree with the biblical account. Their proposals remain an intriguing option to which many believers adhere. Many of their findings, however, have been repudiated by other Christians in the sciences.[10]

Progressive (old earth) creationism. I try to keep two issues distinct these days: evolution and the age of the earth. I can say with a good degree of certainty that we didn't come from apes. I can't say with any degree of certainty how old dinosaur fossils are.

I find no clear statement in Scripture about the age of the earth; so I don't feel any conflict when scientific research yields very old ages. The first chapter of Genesis could teach a young earth—if its six days of creation are literal, twenty-four hour days. But I see clues in the passage itself that lead me to think otherwise.

Augustine first identified the issue around A.D. 400. He argued that the days in Genesis couldn't be normal days, since the sun didn't exist to mark off days until day four. Moreover, the passage itself speaks of all six days as one day. Genesis 2:4 literally reads as follows:

> *These are the genealogical records of the heavens and the earth in their being created on the day the LORD God made the earth and the heavens. (Gen 2:4, author's translation)*

If these are literal days, there's a discrepancy. Are we talking about 144 hours or twenty-four hours? If we insist that the language of *days* be read in the foreign context of a scientific logbook, we're introducing a contradiction into the text that neither God nor Moses intended.

The language of days isn't there to establish the length of time God took preparing the earth for man, but to establish the pattern God set for human civilization to follow. God is pictured as a workman, laboring by

---

comb, whose *Genesis Flood* (Philipsburg, N.J.: Presbyterian & Reformed, 1961) was instrumental in reintroducing young earth creationism into the modern church. Today Morris's organization, The Institute for Creation Research, in San Diego is the center of the young-earth approach.

[10]See Hayward, *Creation*, pp. 114-57, for a number of erroneous creationist arguments. See also Hugh Ross, *Creation & Time: A Biblical and Scientific Perspective on the Creation-Date Controversy* (Colorado Springs: NavPress, 1994), pp. 103-18.

day, sleeping at night and taking a whole day off at the end of the week. These are *God's days,* anthropomorphic days, and not necessarily twenty-four hour periods.[11]

The structure—not the number of minutes—is how the language of days functions within Genesis 1. Of course, the Hebrew word for day *(yom)* does not always refer to a twenty-four hour period elsewhere in Scripture (see, for example, Job 20:28; Ps 20:1; Prov 11:4; 24:10; 25:13; Eccles 7:14).

God may have taken billions of years to prepare the earth for humanity, but he performed a series of direct creative acts, bringing about various kinds of life at different times. This culminated with the creation of Adam, not from a preexisting animal but from nonliving matter.

Reading God's Two Books Together

Within this progressive creation framework, research could be right that the earth is four billion years old. Humanity, however, is a relative newcomer. Skeletons of modern Homo sapiens stretch back into the thousands of years but not the millions of years.

These are ballpark estimates, but biochemical dating based on mutations in mitochondrial DNA has located a biochemical Eve—one woman from whom all women on earth descend—at about fifty thousand years ago. Similar research on the Y-chromosome has identified a biochemical Noah—one man from whom all men descend—at around forty thousand years ago.[12]

There is therefore a unity between God's redemptive book of Scripture and his creational book of nature. They offer different information, but together they complement one another and give a fuller picture.

When we consider what each of the major evolutionary views expects to find in the fossil record, a remarkable similarity arises. The fossil

---

[11]C. John Collins, "How Old Is the Earth? Anthropomorphic Days in Genesis 1:1—2:3," *Presbyterion* 20, no. 2 (1994): 109-30.

[12]For a survey of recent scientific discoveries that may touch on the historicity of Genesis 1—11 from a legitimate source, see Hugh Ross, *The Genesis Question: Scientific Advances and the Accuracy of Genesis* (Colorado Springs: NavPress, 1998).

record reveals the abrupt appearance of the various species, but—over many hundreds of millions of years—stasis following their appearance. The fossil record does not reveal a gradual transformation of one species into another—as traditional Darwinism postulates.

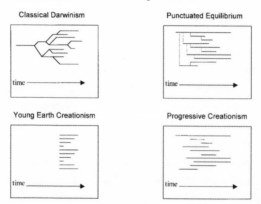

But neither does it reveal the appearance of all species at the same time—as young-earth creationism proposes. Punctuated equilibrium and progressive creationism, however, both predict the same pattern—a pattern the fossil evidence actually confirms. Christians can therefore find room for cooperation with many evolutionary scientists.

There are a couple huge differences between punctuated equilibrium and progressive creation, though. First, creationists actually predicted these results in the fossil record *before* the evidence was accumulated. Progressive creation in some form was the dominant creationist view in the nineteenth century and, if you count Augustine and Anselm (A.D. 1100), is older still. Punctuated equilibrium, by contrast, was developed after the data came in so as to explain the embarrassing lack of evidence for Darwinism.

The other big difference relates to causality. Both agree that species suddenly appear on earth. The evolutionary side argues that evolution took place too rapidly to leave evidence. The creationist side says *hogwash*. A miracle is more believable that an argument from silence and a string of hypothetical mutations so radical as to stretch the natural limits of biological change to the breaking point.

God is not a God of contradictions but of truth. Both of his books can be misinterpreted. Indeed, God's books correct misreading in both directions. Our God has spoken to us in both his books, and we do well to humbly read both together in dependence on him who is the source of truth and wisdom.

Questions for Discussion

1. A friend tells you that Christianity and science cannot coexist since religion is always hostile to free thinking. How might you respond?

2. What are God's two books? Where does Scripture discuss them?

3. Read Genesis 2:19-20. Is this passage about more than how chickens got their name? Why? How is it significant?

4. In what ways are the sciences dependent on God?

5. What moral issues do science and technology raise today? How do you think God's law speaks to them?

6. What are four unanswered questions for Darwinian evolution?

7. What different approaches have Christians taken to reconcile God's two books on the creation-evolution issue?

8

A MOST
SPIRITUAL TOPIC

Sex & Sexuality
According to God

*"The man and his wife were both naked,
and they felt no shame."*
GENESIS 2:25

Sexual issues make us Christians feel guiltier than any other area of
sin. Before I became a Christian, one of the first biblical passages I
read was the Sermon on the Mount. What a place for a young man
to start! Right after Jesus says that lust violates the command against adultery, he says if your eye causes you to sin, pluck it out (Mt 5:28-29).
Thankfully, I never actually cut a hand off or plucked out an eyeball. Our
sexuality seems so riddled with guilt and shame; it's tempting to demon-
ize sexuality itself.

At times Christians have done just that. In the early centuries more
than one monk castrated himself and fled to the desert. Augustine, in
opposition, thought sex within marriage could honor God—just so long
as the participants were trying to make a baby and didn't enjoy it. Plato
called the body an evil that deforms the soul—a view that affected Christian attitudes toward the body and sexuality for centuries.

God Invented Sex

Before the Fall, before anybody ever sinned, before there was any guilt or shame, God made our bodies—genitalia included—and instructed us to "be fruitful and increase in number" (Gen 1:28). God taught our first parents about sex. We weren't designed to reproduce by spores. God invented sex and said it was "very good" (Gen 1:31).

Even after sixteen centuries and a sexual revolution, Christians still often feel like sex is bad. Perhaps C. S. Lewis was right when he suggested that the Fall had a bigger impact on our sexuality than on most areas. Few people put up posters of food on their walls. You can't download illicit images of the "freshest cabbage legally available" for a monthly fee. Because our sexuality is messed up, it's easy to miss the holy character God gives it at creation.

Scripture has harsh words for those who would vilify these gifts:

> [S]ome will abandon the faith and follow deceiving spirits and things taught by demons. Such teachings come from hypocritical liars, whose consciences have been seared as with a hot iron. They forbid people to marry and order them to abstain from certain foods, which God created to be received with thanksgiving by those who believe and who know the truth. For everything God created is good, and nothing is to be rejected if it is received with thanksgiving, because it is consecrated by the word of God and prayer. (1 Tim 4:1-5)

Notice the apostle's concern to uphold the goodness of creation. Saying our sexuality is an evil thing comes from demons and deceiving spirits. Sexuality is a good gift to be received with thankful voices, prayerful hearts and biblically saturated minds.

We Don't Value Sex Enough

Our world misunderstands the true nature of sexual sin. People don't fall into sexual sin because they value sex too highly. They value sex too lowly. Were I to throw around money unwisely, paying fifteen dollars for a cup of coffee, no one would tell me I value money too highly. But when a man gives away sexual intimacy to every woman he meets, the world assumes he really loves sex. *Wrong.* He despises sex. He's treating God's good gift like something cheap.

To devalue God's gifts—like Esau devalued his birthright, trading it for a bowl of stew—is godlessness. Scripture makes this connection: "See that no one is sexually immoral, or is godless like Esau, who for a single meal sold his inheritance rights as the oldest son" (Heb 12:16). Sexual sin is a failure to accept with thankfulness the high value God places upon sex as part of his holy creation order.

We live in a culture focused on the letter of the law more than on its spirit. When an American president can deny an extramarital affair based on an interpretation of the word *is,* we know we've missed the spirit of the law. It would be easy to simply ask, *What are the biblical rules for sex?* But if we approach it this way, we miss what the Bible actually teaches about sexuality.

If I can introduce a big word, we need to ask the *teleological* question—from the Greek word *telos,* meaning "end" or "purpose." This question takes us back to God's design. In other words, we should ask, *What was God's original intent for sexual relationships?*

This is the one question whose answer explains all the other questions. If we simply tell Christians what not to do, while failing to offer a greater vision for what God says sexuality can be, then we fail in our calling to see the world as God sees it. To tell us to "just say no" doesn't give the motivation to keep from being polluted by immorality.

When we grasp the positive sexual vision God gives us, the sinful imitation loses its luster. I remember hearing about a man who investigated counterfeit currency for the federal government. Asked if he spent hours studying different kinds of counterfeit money, he replied, "No. We just learn what a real hundred dollar bill looks like. When you know what the real thing is, the fakes all become obvious." What is the "real thing"?

At creation God gives us the pattern for sexual relationships: one man and one woman within the secure bond of a monogamous, life-long heterosexual marriage—a covenant focused on serving God and caring for one another. This is authentic sexuality, sexuality designed and defined by God. Genesis 2 presents the real thing:

*But for Adam no suitable helper was found. So the LORD God caused the man
to fall into a deep sleep; and while he was sleeping, he took one of the man's
ribs and closed up the place with flesh. Then the LORD God made a woman
from the rib he had taken out of the man, and he brought her to the man.*
   The man said,

> *"This is now bone of my bones*
> *and flesh of my flesh;*
> *she shall be called 'woman,'*
> *for she was taken out of man."*

*For this reason a man will leave his father and mother and be united to his
wife, and they will become one flesh.*
   The man and the woman were both naked, and they felt no shame.
   (Gen 2:20-25)

The creation of woman resolves the first weakness in the Bible.
Before sin entered the world, God condemned one thing: human isola-
tion: "It is not good for the man to be alone" (Gen 2:18). So God made a
woman, a helper suitable for him—literally, *a helper according to his
complement.*

Unlike the modern notion of independent individuals making marriage
contracts to further their own best interests, God designed us as dependent
people to live in union with another in a relationship characterized by
mutual giving. The man and the woman were made for each other.

God designed the physical, sexual union of husband and wife to
reflect this deeper spiritual union by which they give themselves to each
other. "The wife's body does not belong to her alone but also to her husband. In the same way, the husband's body does not belong to him
alone but also to his wife" (1 Cor 7:4). The context in which God gives
his good gift of sex is a secure covenant of self-giving, a willingness to
live for someone outside oneself in the service of God in holy union
under him. This is the only context in which sex is designed to satisfy.

The pattern God set for real sex is one man and one woman express-
ing total commitment. Sex is not authentic with competition and perfor-
mance-based love, if it's about getting rather than giving. It is a lie if our
actions say I love you while our hearts say I love myself.

It's no surprise that so many people in dishonorable sexual relationships think it feels so right. Most lies do feel good. A lonely person enjoys thinking, *Someone loves me, values me and is committed to me.* But it's all a sham. The love, value and commitment—what we call *marriage*—aren't really there. The outward form of sex is there, but it's only self-seeking genital contact, an ultimately unsatisfying fraud that hurts rather than heals.

I've never spoken to someone who regretted being faithful to his or her spouse, nor anyone who regretted postponing sex until marriage. No one ever regrets sexual purity. But I've met lots of people who regret their sexual sin. Truth sets us free, but lies leave us in bondage.

God's Yes Leads to God's No

Even in our culture God's commands speak powerfully, prohibiting sins like premarital sex, adultery, divorce, homosexual behavior, bestiality and lust. But these commandments are not arbitrary. What makes sexual sin sinful is that it detracts from the glorious vision God gives us for what sexuality can be. It values sex too little.

Throughout the Bible, any deviation from God's pattern receives condemnation. Sex before marriage is condemned as a "disgraceful" thing in the Mosaic code (Deut 22:20-21). Jesus identifies sexual immorality as one of the things that makes a person unclean (Mt 15:19). Paul prohibits it because it unites our bodies with someone who is neither spouse nor Lord (1 Cor 6:15-20).

Adultery similarly mars God's beautiful vision. In ancient Israel, God required both the man and woman caught in adultery to be executed (Deut 22:22). Again, what's missing is the spiritual union between husband and wife, making the sex act a forgery. Adultery's evil lies in its failure to honor marriage (Heb 13:4).

Divorce, as a breaking of the marriage covenant, is similarly a form of adultery, which God says he hates (Mal 2:16). When Jesus prohibited divorce he didn't say divorce breaks a rule, but that it breaks a vision. Unless the marriage is already destroyed by adultery, Jesus explains, divorce violates God's design for marriage (Mt 19:3-9). Scripture forbids other behaviors that deviate from the creation pattern: bestiality (Ex 22:19), which "defiles" a person (Lev 18:23), and incest (Deut 27:20-23).

God's great vision for sex is similarly distorted by homosexual sin. Again, God's condemnation is not arbitrary. Homosexual acts exchange the "natural" pattern for an "unnatural" one (Rom 1:26). Paul isn't addressing here whether a genetic factor is involved in homosexual temptation. Rather, he's saying that homosexual sin violates the nature of sex as God created it.

The fact that homosexuality breaks God's design is borne out by the unbelievable promiscuity within the gay community. Studies of gay men, for example, have found that the large majority report more than fifty previous sexual partners.[1] Men simply cannot answer the God-given neediness of the male heart.

Another sexual topic single or married believers often ask about is masturbation. The issue is complicated by the lack of a direct biblical reference. Attempts to identify Onan's sin as masturbation are off base (Gen 38:8-10). Onan "spilled his semen on the ground" to avoid the responsibility of providing descendants for his dead brother—abandoning a God-given duty within ancient Israel (Deut 25:5-6).

It would be tempting to conclude that, since the Bible doesn't mention masturbation, it must be okay. But we shouldn't ask, "Is there a biblical rule against masturbation?" Rather, we should ask, "Does masturbation fulfill the vision for sex that God gives at creation?" In this light, I doubt a Christian can justify a habit of masturbation. Still, in the absence of a specific biblical prohibition, I don't dwell on the issue.

What the Bible dwells on is lust, the real issue behind masturbation. The Holy Spirit aims at our hearts as well as our bodies. Lust is a violation of God's design for our sexuality, as the Scripture warns, "Do not lust in your heart after her beauty" (Prov 6:25). Jesus called lust a heart form of adultery (Mt 5:29). Lust—whether or not it accompanies mastur-

---

[1]R. A. Kaslow et al., "The Multicenter AIDS Cohort Study: Rationale, Organization, and Selected Characteristics of the Participants," *American Journal of Epidemiology* 126, no. 2 (1987): 310-18.

bation—is self-aggrandizing, while God's design for sex is all about giving rather than taking.

I've known of people who think masturbation is more pleasurable
than intercourse. It's no surprise, since masturbation doesn't require you
to care about anyone but yourself. It's easier to make love to an imagi-
nary person who exists for your pleasure than to actually love a real person. There's no shortcut to true intimacy. Lasting intimacy requires
becoming a giver.

When we ask the right question—What can our sexuality be by God's
design?—we come face to face with a stunning vision. It's a picture of
men and women committed and giving to one another, looking out for
the interests of one another more than themselves. It's sexual intimacy
within an intimate relationship of love and acceptance. It's safe, secure
and stable. This is sex according to God. His powerful yes. All God's
noes about sex simply guard this one overwhelming yes.

If He's Not a Porn Addict, He's Probably Gay

Recent decades have seen biblical Christians really beginning to deal
with the fact that sex is a good gift of God. At the same time, though,
many Christian leaders have found that sexual sin has a stronger strangle-
hold on Christian churches than ever before.

A friend of mine who's a pastor and I have noticed a sharp rise in
both homosexual sin and pornography—particularly through the Internet. When he started a new church, he found himself spending far more
time than he'd ever imagined counseling Christian men who'd struggled
with homosexual temptation and never told a soul, Christian women
who'd secretly lived lesbian lifestyles, couples on the brink of divorce
because husbands were addicted to pornography. *Lots* of husbands were
addicted to pornography. After we'd compared notes the thought was
voiced, "If he's not a porn addict, he's probably gay."

Our society has sought sexual gratification to blunt the pain of being
isolated and lonely. The pornography industry has blossomed from a $10
million a year industry in 1973 to a $10 billion industry today—that's a
thousandfold increase. And sexual sin is remarkably addictive. The vision

God gives at creation seems impossible to us, so ingrained is our selfishness and so stubborn our habits of sin.

A few figures throughout the history of the church have tried to argue that the sin in the Garden was sexual intercourse. That's *dumb*. But sexuality does become a big issue immediately after the Fall. "Then the eyes of them both were opened, and they realized they were naked; so they sewed fig leaves together and made coverings for themselves" (Gen 3:7).

Though the serpent had promised them they'd know good and evil, he hadn't warned them they'd know evil by being enslaved to it. Their first sensation was less one of enlightenment and more one of shame. Their eyes were opened, sure—but to their own nakedness. Our first parents hid themselves from God, saying, "I was afraid because I was naked" (Gen 3:10).

It's an odd thing to say to God. Adam and Eve had always been naked. How did they know what nakedness was? Why did they suddenly feel unclothed? They suddenly sensed a lack within themselves, a feeling of vulnerability, an embarrassment they hadn't known before. So they tried to cover it up.

Their sexuality was a window into their souls, and their souls needed covering. Before, God had covered them with righteousness and holiness. They had been worthy. Now, all that was lost. As soon as we fell, our sexuality became the focus of our shame.

Healing a Sexually Sickened Creation

God can heal our sexually shattered lives. I've watched sexually immoral men become faithful husbands and fathers. I've seen women struggling against lesbian temptations become faithful wives. I've known men who used to lust after other men who do so no longer. I've known others who still struggle but who really *struggle* without giving up. I've known men enslaved to habits of lust and masturbation and pornography find substantial freedom. None of this has been their doing. The difference between these men and women and the millions still enslaved to sin has been the sanctifying power of God's Spirit.

Fifty years from now, if you're still alive, what kind of person will you be? What kind of character are you developing: one that yields to God or resists him? Only God can change our hearts, but Scripture warns us that God's Spirit can be quenched. What must we do to see sin's power broken and our lives transformed?

1. We have to realize what sexual sin is. It is sin, which means it's in opposition to God. I knew a young man in college who wanted desperately to overcome homosexual temptation. He hated the fact that something had control over him. So he looked to Christianity to strengthen him in his battle for self-control. That lasted about a year, and then he left the faith, identified himself as an atheist, and entered the gay lifestyle. He never really wanted God; he just wanted self-control. Do you want to overcome sexual sin because you love the Lord? The heart issue isn't behavior modification. The heart issue is God.

It's important that we learn to grieve over our sin. A lot of Christians think that because God has forgiven their sin, they shouldn't feel bad when some pattern of sin has their hearts. That's a big mistake and, if followed too long, can harden their heart toward the Spirit's convicting power. Feeling bad for sin is not necessarily a sign of legalism. If you're thinking you have to clean up your act for God to like you, that's legalism. If you feel guilty for doing something God gives you freedom to do, that's legalism. But if you feel dirty and broken because you're trapped in sin, but you know by faith that God loves you and are ready to trust him to help you, that's called a healthy Christian life.

Jesus tells us that those whose spirits are poor are blessed—as are those who mourn over their spiritual poverty and are therefore meek. God's kingdom, his comfort and promise of a future life all give a deep happiness of soul, a blessedness that comes not from being a good boy or girl but from belonging to God. So long as you're hungry for something you haven't yet attained, you can know God's blessing is upon you—and he promises that you "will be filled" (Mt 5:3-6).

2. We need to learn true worship. This may sound odd, but sexual sin—like all sin—is at heart a dysfunction of worship. We are, by nature, religious creatures, and when our hearts turn from the true God, we instinctively seek out a substitute god. Sexual sin flows from a heart that cheapens sex, but then seeks satisfaction in sex as if it were God.

At the same time, though, the very problem is itself a judgment from God. Our sexual desires seem so out of line with God's design in creation because God is punishing the human race for its idolatry. The apostle writes:

> *They exchanged the truth of God for a lie, and worshiped and served created things rather than the Creator—who is forever praised. Amen.*
> *Because of this, God gave them over to shameful lusts. (Rom 1:25-26)*

When our hearts seek their satisfaction in the creation rather than the Creator, God says, "Fine—I'll give you enough rope to hang yourselves." Sexual healing requires that we be trained again in the proper worship of God. A heart trained to delight in God finds the promises of sin unimpressive.

3. Since we're the rebels, sexual wholeness must begin with repentance and forgiveness. We won't see God's purifying power in our lives unless we stand before him as broken and needy sinners. God has obligated himself to receive every repentant sinner who comes to him in Christ. "Come to me, all you who are weary and burdened," Jesus promises, "and I will give you rest" (Mt 11:28). When we look at the sinners Jesus most welcomed—like the prostitute (Lk 7:36-50)—they approached him knowing their sin and seeking his mercy.

Are you hungry for righteousness in your life? If so, Jesus says you are blessed (Mt 5:6). It's the spiritually poor who belong to the kingdom of heaven and those who mourn their sin whom God comforts (Mt 5:3-4). The man who prayed about how good he was didn't leave right with God, but the one who beat his breast and cried "God, have mercy on me, a sinner" went home righteous in God's sight—not because he wallowed in his sin but because he approached God as one needy for mercy and hungry for grace (Lk 18:9-14).

4. We overcome sexual sin as we learn to claim God's promises. The Bible doesn't point us inward to see change happen but always outward to Jesus Christ and his promises. Rarely does Scripture give a command without a promise. We don't live by the bare commands of God's law but by the grace of the God who gives us his law.

The key to freedom is not our faithfulness to God but his faithfulness to us—and our willingness to believe God, to trust him for the strength to obey even five more seconds. We don't sin because we're using too much grace; we sin when we use too little. Sin won't be our master precisely because we are not under law but under grace (Rom 6:14).

Hear God's promise alongside his command:

> No temptation has seized you except what is common to man. And God is faithful; he will not let you be tempted beyond what you can bear. But when you are tempted, he will provide a way out so that you can stand up under it. (1 Cor 10:13)

The command—to obey—isn't even explicitly stated here. Instead we see God's powerful promise that you will never be in a situation where you have to dishonor him. Never. He swears he will curb the temptation to the level you need it in order to obey. When we fail, it's because we don't believe what God is promising. But we'll learn to stand when we learn to take all the grace we're offered.

5. *Most of all, though, sexual change requires God to do something.* Neither you nor I have the strength to combat the wickedness in our souls. God requires us to put to death the misdeeds of our sinful nature—that's our job (Col 3:5). But he also knows that we can only do this because our lives are now hidden with Christ in God (Col 3:3). God must change our hearts.

Scripture tells us to be filled with the Holy Spirit moment-by-moment. "Do not get drunk on wine, which leads to debauchery. Instead, be filled with the Spirit" (Eph 5:18). To be filled means to be controlled or driven by something—like being "filled with jealousy" (Acts 5:17) or being "filled with compassion" (Lk 15:20). To be filled with the Holy Spirit is to be empowered, motivated and controlled by God at work in our hearts.

How can you do that? In a backhanded way Scripture says you can't. To be filled with the Spirit is a direction to have someone else do something. It's as if I commanded you to be given a million dollars. You may be willing, but someone else must act on your behalf. God commands you to have the Holy Spirit do something. How?

Theologians through the ages have identified certain *means of grace*, highways along which the Holy Spirit travels. If you want God to work in your life, he has his favorite roads. In an almost identical passage to the Ephesians command "Be filled with the Spirit," Paul substitutes the instruction "Let the word of Christ dwell in you richly" (Col 3:16). The point of the comparison is that we're brought under the Spirit's control as God's word fills our minds.

There are other highways of the Spirit. The classic means of grace are the *Word of God, prayer,* and the *sacraments* of baptism and the Lord's Supper, which visibly symbolize and seal God's promises to us. I'd also add the *discipline of our brothers and sisters in the church*—be it their encouragement or their rebuke or even censure (Mt 18:15-20). We seek the Lord by meditating on his Word (Ps 1:2), impressing it on our hearts (Deut 6:6), talking about it (Deut 6:7), and listening to it read, taught and preached (2 Tim 4:2). "I have hidden your word in my heart," the psalmist exclaims, "that I might not sin against you" (Ps 119:11).

And the Lord hears us when we call to him in prayer. It doesn't matter how many minutes you pray (Mt 6:7-8). Pray alone (Mt 6:6). Pray with other believers (1 Thess 3:10). Get church leaders praying for you (Jas 5:14). Pray formal prayers like the one Jesus taught (Mt 6:9-13). Or just tell God what's on your heart. But pray continually (1 Thess 5:17).

The relationship is what counts—not the lingo. God wants to know you, promises to listen (1 Jn 5:14-15), and gives his children good gifts (Mt 6:7-11). You aren't just talking to air. Pray for things God wants: like righteousness, opportunities to serve, protection for church leaders and for his will to be done on earth. But don't let your spiritual life revolve around one particular area of struggle.

And—this is key—give yourself to a group of Christians, to a church. Augustine reminds us that the church isn't a club for saints but a hospital for sinners. The church is the primary context in which we see the means of grace—Scripture, prayer and sacraments—operating in the New Testament (Acts 2:42). Secret sins are the least willing to loosen their grip. Tell a couple believers who can encourage you when you're weak, rebuke you when you're stubborn, check up on you from time to time, and in every way point you to your Father who gives you his promises to live by.

A Sexless Sexual Future

We're naive if we think that sexuality has its only outlet in sexual acts. Sexuality is a larger category than sex itself. Sexuality is a part of our humanness. Jesus, the perfect human, was a sexual man like any other—but without the sin. Still, Jesus never married.

He traveled from town to town for the three years of his earthly ministry (Lk 8:1), didn't own a home (Lk 9:58) and was called to die in his early thirties. Such a ministry can't easily nurture a family. But does this mean Jesus was asexual? Absolutely not. Jesus was a true man, even though he abstained from sex. Jesus displayed his masculinity by providing faithful leadership, self-sacrifice, zeal for God and purity in his dealings with women—but without avoiding women as if they were dangerous!

Abstinence needn't mean sexual repression. There are times when God calls us to give up some pleasure not because it's a bad thing but precisely because it's a good thing. We don't fast because food is bad but because it's good. By giving it up for a time we're saying, "God, I need you more than your gifts." Scripture says that married believers may give up sexual relations temporarily, by mutual consent, in order to pray (1 Cor 7:5).

Jesus taught that some believers are called to give up the right to marry—and by implication the gift of sex—in order to serve God's kingdom (Mt 19:12). God calls singles to singleness so they can invest their lives in other people for God's kingdom. "It is good for a man not to marry," Scripture states (1 Cor 7:1). Singleness and marriage are both gifts from God, Paul explains, "but each man has his own gift from God; one has this gift, another has that" (1 Cor 7:7).

This was the path Paul himself took. "Don't we have the right to take a believing wife along with us, as do the other apostles? . . . But I have not used any of these rights" (1 Cor 9:5, 15). American Christians often unintentionally give their single brothers and sisters a hard time when these married people interrogate singles about why they're still single or when they're getting married. Perhaps they're overreacting to a culture that devalues marriage. Or it may simply be that they've found marriage to be a wonderful blessing and want others to experience it.

Whatever the reason, it's wrong to assume that because God is calling a person to be single that he or she must be either gay or a loser or bitter about it all. God's reasons for Christian singleness revolve around his kingdom (Mt 19:12), so as to serve the Lord unhindered by family commitments (1 Cor 7:32-35). It's vital that we recognize singleness as a gift and empower singles to serve and lead in the church and world as God enables them. After all, we'll all be single one day.

This is a really shocking tidbit Jesus drops. In the future our sexuality is going to be very different. Asked which of her husbands a remarried widow would have in heaven, Jesus responded, "When the dead rise, they will neither marry nor be given in marriage; they will be like the angels in heaven" (Mk 12:25). I wish Jesus had elaborated on this point, but he tells us all we need to know right now. We'll all be as single as Gabriel and Michael someday.

This is astounding because it's the only instance in which something given at creation won't be restored at Christ's return. I have to think that the lack of marriage in heaven won't be a loss, though, but a gain. It's not that you'll love your current spouse less but that you'll love God and everybody else even more. It's a mystery we'll have to wait to comprehend, but we can find sexual wholeness in Christ in this age no matter which gift God gives us. Whether we're called to singleness or the blessings of marriage, he is our model for selfless love as men and women in Christ.

Questions for Discussion

1. What does it mean to say that we don't value sex enough?

2. Why is it not enough just to ask what rules the Bible gives about sex? What question should we ask? Why?

3. Describe the pattern God established at creation. Discuss the relational context in which the gift of sex was given.

4. How do various sexual sins lack this context? What makes these sins sinful?

5. Of the five points under "Healing a Sexually Sickened Creation," which strikes you most? Why?

6. What is the relationship between God's commands and his promises? What might it look like if a Christian were trying to live by the commands rather than the promises?

7. Why does God call some Christians to remain single? Brainstorm some ways you think Christians might better affirm that calling.

9

THE MOST DANGEROUS PART OF THE BODY

Communication According to God

"'You will not surely die,' the serpent said to the woman."
GENESIS 3:4

S ticks and stones may break my bones, but words can hurt me more than any of these. Hit me with a baseball bat, but please don't spread nasty rumors about me. Most sins damage the outside of their victims, but words can hurt the inside. How many times have you stared at the ceiling all night dealing with something someone said?

The Power of Words

"The tongue has the power of life and death," Scripture tells us (Prov 18:21). Words have the power to heal and the power to destroy:

> *The tongue that brings healing is a tree of life,*
> *but a deceitful tongue crushes the spirit. (Prov 15:4)*

James focuses on this inconsistency in human speech:

> *Consider what a great forest is set on fire by a small spark. The tongue also is a fire, a world of evil among the parts of the body. It corrupts the whole person, sets the whole course of his life on fire, and is itself set on fire by hell.*

All kinds of animals, birds, reptiles and creatures of the sea are being
tamed and have been tamed by man, but no man can tame the tongue. It is
a restless evil, full of deadly poison.

With the tongue we praise our Lord and Father, and with it we curse men,
who are made in God's likeness. Out of the same mouth come praise and
cursing. My brothers, this should not be. (Jas 3:5-10)

Lots of people think sexual sin is the most serious sin in the church today. Baloney. Sinful speech kills a lot more churches than sexual sin. Critical words, divisive words, angry words, complaining words, unthankful words—these do more damage than all the affairs in Washington. Adultery is a lot easier to control than criticism. Our words have the power to do more good than our sexuality, but they can also do more damage. The tongue is the most dangerous part of the body.

It wasn't always like this. Communication first went wrong in Eden when the serpent started talking with our first parents. He bypassed the family structure God has created, going directly to the helper Eve rather than to her husband. Then he distorted God's words ever so slightly, asking if God had forbidden eating from *any* tree in the Garden (Gen 3:1). Between the lines you can hear him questioning God's fairness.

Eve began to fall for the deception. God said not to eat from the tree in the middle of the Garden (Gen 2:17), but Eve added that they weren't allowed to *touch* it (Gen 3:3). God hadn't said that. She was starting to believe that God had been unfair, and attempted to justify that thought.

Then the serpent directly contradicted God's words. Should you eat from the forbidden tree, God had promised, "You will surely die" (Gen 2:17). But the serpent promised, "You will *not* surely die" (Gen 3:4, emphasis mine). He lied.

He continued by giving God a motive: God was afraid that they'd rival him if they ate from that tree. And then the serpent clinched the deal. He promised that the humans would become like God (Gen 3:5). So Eve ate the forbidden fruit and gave some to Adam, who ate as well.

Jesus called the devil the father of lies (Jn 8:44), for his lie introduced deception into the human heart. Words are powerful.

Jesus said we'd be judged by our words: "For by your words you will be acquitted, and by your words you will be condemned" (Mt 12:37). Our words, he explained, are the overflow valve on our hearts. "For out of the overflow of the heart the mouth speaks" (Mt 12:34). Our speech reveals what we're really like on the inside, where no one can see.

Words have power to give life or death, to show love or hate. Communication, like sexuality, is a sphere of God's good creation that has painfully seen the effects of the Fall. Yet the Bible warns us about our mouths far more frequently than it does our genitalia. It's our tongues that cause the most trouble.

Why God Gave Us Tongues

Rather than first asking "What biblical rules govern communication?" we instead begin the *teleological* question again. Why did God give us language? Once we understand the purpose communication serves, the rules make sense.

Secular communication theory generally starts with an evolutionary model that imagines language gradually developing to enable us to convey information. Transmitting information is therefore the chief goal. Once God and his design are out of the picture we're left with a shallow vision for our verbal interaction with one another.[1]

The biblical picture is much more compelling. We see communication before the beginning, as God speaks among the persons of the Godhead: "Let us make man in our image" (Gen 1:26). Be it literature or television or just a conversation with a friend over coffee, communication finds its foundation in God himself. Indeed, God's words carried his creative power. He said, "Let there be light," and light sprang into existence (Gen 1:3).

Theologians have said that God created the world *ex nihilo,* "out of nothing." He didn't just assemble the parts. There was no matter from which to fashion the stars—God created the matter itself. But I think the

---

[1]For an excellent Christian introduction to communication, see Quentin J. Schultze, *Communicating for Life: Christian Stewardship in Community and Media* (Grand Rapids, Mich.: Baker, 2000).

biblical picture is that God created the world *ex verba*, "out of words." God's words were the creative force by which he created all things.

The Bible is *logocentric*, "centered on words." Postmodern scholarship has invented a myth that people are, by nature, image-centered, that our word-focused character is an invention of the printing press, which coincided with the rise of biblical fundamentalism. It's a compelling myth to a society wanting freedom from texts like law codes or the Bible.

But look at Plato, Aristotle, the days before either the printing press or Christianity. People were logocentric then too. And the same pattern holds true in China, the ancient Near East, and even primitive cultures where the spoken word took primacy.

Words are a big part of being human. Even in an image-saturated culture with video games and the great American babysitter (television)—children still love books. A focus on words is neither modern nor uniquely Christian. It's human.

God's Three Goals in Communication

Only when we understand people according to God can we understand their communication according to God.

1. Our words display God's glory. We've seen that God made us to glorify himself (1 Cor 10:31)—so our communication has God's glory as its goal. Our speech can display God's goodness or truth. Even the Pharisees who attacked Jesus could use the phrase "give glory to God" as a synonym for telling the truth (Jn 9:24). Lying is wrong because it goes against God's character: "God is not a man, that he should lie" (Num 23:19). It's impossible for him to lie (Heb 6:18).

Our words can also display God's beauty. Our mouths can offer praise, adoration and commitment to God. They can extol him above his creation, value him above his gifts. "My mouth will speak in praise of the LORD" (Ps 145:21).

2. Our words build civilization. And human communication is not only understood in light of the purpose for which God made us but also in light of the calling God gave us. The cultural mandate to establish human civilization (Gen 1:28) requires language. Even in naming the animals we see Adam using language (Gen 2:19-20). Language is an indispensable foundation for the cultural mandate.

Consider what an affront to human society a simple lie can become. A false or hurtful tongue damages and cheapens speech itself. "Talk is cheap," people say. But God didn't design it that way. We make words cheap when they mean nothing. That's why the Savior taught us to let our yes mean yes and our no mean no (Mt 5:33-37). We shouldn't even have to give an oath or a promise. A friend doesn't ask you to promise unless you've let her down in the past. Promises only exist because words are already among the wounded.

3. Our words reflect God's image. Human communication also reflects the position God gave us as his image bearers upon the earth (Gen 1:27). Before God made us in his image, he was speaking (Gen 1). Granted, our words don't have the same power to shape reality as God's. But as creatures that bear God's image, our ability to communicate as God communicates sets us apart from the world of beasts.

Every aspect of God's image in us—rationality, creativity, righteousness, community, dominion—involves the ability to communicate. Through language we can reason out complex issues and understand implications for various courses of action. Language has long been a favorite for human creativity. In the English language alone just think of Chaucer, Shakespeare, Faulkner and Eliot.

Think of the relational aspect of God's image. Hugs are wonderful, but imagine how lonely a relationship would be without words. Communication permits us to get into another person's heart and let others into ours.

Speaking Love and Life into People

It's the relational quality of God's image being served by communication that we see most clearly in Scripture. Within this framework, words are God's vehicles of love to one another.

God gives us the good gift of communication so we can encourage one another. We don't just talk; *we communicate life and love to one another.* This is so central to God's vision that Scripture calls us to say *only* that which encourages other people.

Do not let any unwholesome talk come out of your mouths, but only what is helpful for building others up *according to their needs, that it may benefit those who listen. (Eph 4:29, emphasis mine)*

A legalistic approach to communication assumes that we can say whatever we like so long as it doesn't break a rule. Legalism, while always presenting itself as a holier standard to live by, is always a looser standard than Scripture since it bypasses the deceptive issues of the heart.

We don't say anything at all, God tells us, except that which encourages others. Imagine a world in which people always thought about their words first, a world in which people only opened their mouths to edify one another, a world of deliberate life-giving speech. Every time we open our mouths, we have an opportunity to "look not only to [our] own interests, but also to the interests of others" (Phil 2:4).

Which is more important from God's perspective: truth or love? It's not a good idea to set the two in opposition—God is both. But when information and love conflict, love must prevail. Even angelic tongues are worthless if not driven by love (1 Cor 13:1). As important as truthfulness is in our communication (Deut 5:20), the primary purpose for which God gave us language is to convey life-giving love.

Think of the Hebrew midwives. Pharaoh commanded them to kill all the Jewish baby boys at birth, but the midwives refused, telling a far-fetched tale about Jewish women delivering babies before the midwives arrive (Ex 1:15-21). God seems to be sanctioning a lie.

While God directs us not to lie, the overarching goal of communication is to transfer life—not just information. The midwives loved God and loved the babies; therefore, they transferred inaccurate information so that they could also transfer life. Pharaoh's goal was to do evil against God and humanity. So God called the midwives to speak life, even if it meant deception—and God blessed them for their faithfulness (Ex 1:21). Similarly, Rahab lied about the Jewish spies she was hiding (Josh 2:2-6), an act for which she was engrafted into Israel as a woman of God.

There are only a few instances in which it's not a sin to lie. But when the accurate transfer of information conflicts with the transfer of life and love, love prevails. Love is God's purpose for communication. By contrast, there is never a reason for us to speak hate toward God or neighbor. Love for God and for his image in man is God's prime directive for human communication.

When Not to Speak

Sometimes we speak love by not speaking at all. I'm convinced that the most important tool in developing relationships is listening. This takes a lot of effort. "He who answers before listening—that is his folly and shame" (Prov 18:13). To really hear what someone is saying involves putting yourself into their shoes, understanding their struggles.

I remember a conversation with a man who worked as a painter in my apartment building—we'll call him Jeff. I talked with Jeff while he was painting one day. He knew I had gone to seminary and asked why I'd be into something like church. I told him a little about my own conversion to Christ, and he seemed intrigued. After a while I got up the guts to ask, "Do you have any church background?"

Jeff's answer was unexpected: "I don't go to church because I'm gay." A few years earlier I might have launched into a lecture about God's design for sexuality, but the Lord had been teaching me to listen. I just said, "Man. That must be tough." And I looked him in the eye, pursed my lips in display of empathy and said nothing. My silence was inviting him to share his life.

Jeff told me his story. I learned about the rejection he got from his parents, and how a former boyfriend's dad, a minister, had accepted Jeff as a son. That pastor, he said, thought that homosexuality was perfectly fine. Jeff assumed I would too. I didn't, but again I listened rather than speaking.

What was I to say? The only "religious" person who hadn't rejected Jeff was a liberal pastor who didn't believe the Bible. Eventually we talked about how Jesus calls Christians both to love and to speak the truth. We talked about how Jesus tells us God's law still forbids homosexual practices, that gay sex isn't God's design.

We talked about former homosexuals in the New Testament church (1 Cor 6:11) and about the difference between homosexual temptation and action. We talked about Jesus saving sinners like us.

When Jeff told me that he couldn't live without sex, I told him that sex seemed a small sacrifice. What we seek in sex is intimacy, and gay sex is notorious—even in the gay community—for lacking intimacy. Jeff probably had more intimacy sharing his life story with me than he experienced in fifty gay relationships.

I don't know where Jeff is now, either geographically or spiritually. But the last time I spoke with him he was visiting a Bible-based church. I could see my words breathing life into him, but I think my silence was what had been instrumental. The fact that I listened to Jeff, understood him and didn't judge him spoke more loudly than when I explicitly told him he needed to come to Jesus Christ in faith and repentance.

When we speak primarily to show how much we know, force our perspective on another or "solve" someone else's problem when they just want to talk about it, we aren't speaking love and life into them. "Everyone should be quick to listen, slow to speak and slow to become angry" (Jas 1:19). Relationships are what matters. Speech is just a tool.

This is also why it's not always okay to say something just because it's true. Take gossip. The lady in the pew behind you may have cussed when she missed the traffic light pulling into church. That doesn't mean you should talk about it. You'd just hurt her. "A perverse man stirs up dissention, / and a gossip separates close friends" (Prov 16:28). When we talk about other people's weaknesses, we may be speaking the truth, but we're not "speaking the truth in love" (Eph 4:15). And love is the standard God gives us, more important than either hope or faith (1 Cor 13:13).

Even when we have to confront a fellow Christian's sin, the same goal of speaking life and love into them stands. We don't rebuke people for every sin they commit. Love first of all covers over a multitude of sins (Prov 10:12) and keeps no record of wrongs (1 Cor 13:5). If we have to confront a brother or sister in Christ and feel like they're bad and we need to tell them off, we should examine whether we're living by God's grace at all.

The Life-Giving Rebuke

There's a nasty myth that says you should always tell someone when you're mad at them. The "I just need to vent" approach to communication. God does not give this counsel. God's standard is to rebuke only *sins*. If we can't show a person which commandment they broke, then we have no business talking to them about their actions.

Jesus taught, "If your brother sins against you, go and show him his fault, just between the two of you. If he listens to you, you have won your brother over" (Mt 18:15). You have to go and show him his fault—literally, the text says to "prove" to him his fault. Helping them see how they violated God's word can win them over.

Even then, we only rebuke sins where repentance is absent, like when there's evidence of a habit. If they're already repentant, a rebuke only condemns—God has already restored them. Thus we forgive seventy-seven times (Mt 18:22). Further, we only offer a rebuke when we're ready to help in overcoming the sin. Again, love is the purpose for all communication, and love "always protects" (1 Cor 13:7). Scripture calls this a *life-giving* rebuke. "He who listens to a life-giving rebuke / will be at home among the wise" (Prov 15:31). To approach a friend and put your finger on his or her sin isn't easy, but even such hard words can flow from love and breathe life into them.

I can pinpoint several rebukes I've received that really breathed spiritual life into me. One came from a friend who rebuked me for trying to control people. Another came from a woman who pulled me aside after a church meeting and showed me how I had used my words to hurt and discourage. I hadn't noticed how sin had my tongue, but these rebukes were spoken in love, proven with Scripture, and led to deep repentance and Christian growth in my life. Words of love are also words of life.

When your church makes a decision you think unwise, or your spouse says something to hurt you, there are two unbelieving paths we can easily take.

When things don't go our way, we can *withdraw*. We may withdraw our words (the "silent treatment"), our finances, our spiritual gifts or our very presence: "I'm outta here." This is the flight in the fight or flight impulse.

While some of us tend to withdraw, others are prone to *criticize*—to fight. We use our words to malign the reputations, wisdom or character of others. And criticism almost always seeks to create a faction. "If we can get half the church mad about this, then they'll have to listen."

But when Paul discusses the acts of the sinful nature, he lists *discord*, *dissensions* and *factions* right in between *witchcraft* and *orgies* (Gal 5:20). "Do everything without complaining or arguing," Scripture instructs (Phil 2:14). Love is what determines what we say and leave unsaid.

The Double-Minded Person

Words, like sticks and stones, can hurt people. But as early as the fourth century Augustine noted that when a person lies the worst damage is to the liar himself. Deceptive words create a division between our inner and outer selves. We become fractured, double people. As lying becomes easier, there become two of me rather than just one. Such is true about all our speech.

When we set forth a front with our words—a separate person from our true selves, often one we create to impress others—we become double-minded and unstable at the soul level. Our words influence our souls. Poorly spoken words inflict their destructive power on the character of the speaker, even if they hurt no one else.

This is the warning James gives us about unbelieving prayers:

> *But when he asks, he must believe and not doubt, because he who doubts is like a wave of the sea, blown and tossed by the wind. That man should not think he will receive anything from the Lord; he is a double-minded man, unstable in all he does. (Jas 1:6-8)*

There are lots of ways a double mind can manifest itself. James mentions half-hearted prayers where the heart and tongue don't line up. Augustine spoke of lying. Hiding behind a curtain of silence can do the same—good, quiet person on the outside, festering bitterness on the inside.

The wisdom God gives is characterized by a unity of heart and tongue. "A wise man's heart guides his mouth, / and his lips promote instruction" (Prov 16:23). The psalmist even expresses a holy hatred of double-minded men (Ps 119:113). He hates them in the sense that he doesn't want to be surrounded by them. A righteous indignation at the two-faced is not always a bad thing. But when we look in the mirror, is the person we see the same as the one we hear in our hearts? I think to some extent we've all become double-minded people.

The Restoring Power of God's Word of Life

Who can tame the tongue? James talks about how all sorts of animals have been domesticated, but no one has mastered his tongue (Jas 3:7-9). Horses were easy, dogs a breeze and cats a little trickier, but still we did it. Our mouths, though, are a different story. If the tongue is going to be tamed, God has to tame it.

God's word gives us a revolutionary new paradigm for our speech. Every time our mouths open, we have an opportunity to change the universe by lovingly speaking life into other people, to display God's perfections, to build civilization and reflect his image in us. This is God's purpose for our mouths. It's a stunning vision but one we'll never attain on our own.

The good news, of course, is that we aren't on our own anymore. As believers, we're now "hidden with Christ in God" (Col 3:3), have life rather than death (Jn 5:24) and are brothers of an unashamed Jesus (Heb 2:11). Christ purchased a radical renewal for our tongues.

We often mistakenly limit Christ's saving work to our forgiveness. He lived and died to do a lot more. He sacrificed himself for us also to tame our tongues.

For God did not appoint us to suffer wrath but to receive salvation through our Lord Jesus Christ. He died for us so that, whether we are awake or asleep,

we may live together with him. Therefore encourage one another and build
each other up, just as in fact you are doing. (1 Thess 5:9-11)

Our words to each other are closely tied to the cross. Jesus came and
died so we'd be *together* with him as a people with domesticated
tongues. God's saving grace puts us into a redeemed community. We
encourage one another now because Jesus redeemed us in the past, is
giving us salvation in the present, and has promised to knit us together
with him and each other both now and in the age to come.

Breaking with hurtful patterns of communication is the flip side of the
coin of new life in Christ.

But now you must rid yourselves of all such as these: anger, rage, malice,
slander and filthy language from your lips. Do not lie to each other, since
you have taken off your old self and have put on the new self, which is being
renewed in knowledge in the image of its Creator. (Col 3:8-10)

Domesticating the tongue is a part of God's great work of image restoration.

I live in a historic neighborhood deep in the city, and I often see old
buildings being restored. While a major part of restoration involves putting in new wiring, plumbing and finishes, a lot of trash also needs to be
removed: rotted wood, broken plaster, orange shag carpeting someone
glued to the wood floors in the 1970s. This is what God is doing to his
image in you and me.

Remove the anger—that doesn't belong. Get rid of the foul language and
the truth stretching. Still, while we have to get rid of these things, the restoration is God's work. We aren't renewing ourselves; we are being renewed.

There's no more powerful testimony of God's grace than a mouth
gripped by the Holy Spirit—a tongue tamed by Jesus Christ. "Let your
conversation be always full of grace, seasoned with salt," Scripture says
(Col 4:6). The mystery is that when our words have failed, God's word
does what our words could not. God says:

So is my word that goes out from my mouth:
    It will not return to me empty,

but will accomplish what I desire
and achieve the purpose for which I sent it. (Is 55:11)

God's word does what he gave it to do—to breath life into us so that our words can breathe life into others.

Ultimately, it's God's word that transforms our words, showing us his love and giving us his life. Indeed, Jesus himself is the Word of life that communicates to us fellowship with God (1 Jn 1:1-3). Through him our communication can bring God glory as we establish civilization through his image in us, by speaking encouragement, life and love to one another.

Questions for Discussion

1. How have you seen words bring the power of life? How have you seen them bring the power of death? Mention specific examples.

2. Why do you think the author says sins of the tongue do more harm even than sexual sin?

3. Read Genesis 3. In what ways do we see speech abused in the Garden?

4. For what reason(s) did God give us communication?

5. How would a legalist approach biblical communication differently? Do you think it makes a difference? Why or why not?

6. How should we deal with someone who sins against us? What should we do, and what should our attitude be?

7. Describe a double-minded person. How can God's grace help us overcome sinful speech and the double-minded heart?

10

No Damnation Without Representation

The Human Condition According to God

"So the LORD God banished him from the Garden of Eden."
GENESIS 3:23

Imagine you're talking to some guy at Starbucks about Jesus Christ. He asks, "You aren't saying people go to hell because they don't share your religion, are you?" You answer, "It's not about me or my religion. Jesus says people go to hell without him." He sucks in about sixteen gallons of air. His face turns red. Then he demands, "So what about the innocent native in Africa who's never heard about Jesus?"

You could point out that sub-Saharan Africa is one of the most Christian parts of the globe. For example, a third of the people of Kenya say they've been born again. But the guy at Starbucks probably isn't so concerned about people in Africa. He's probably more concerned about himself—whether *he* will have to account for what he's done with his life.

The Hunt for the Innocent Native
What about the innocent native in Brooklyn? Would God condemn

someone to eternal punishment for never hearing about Jesus? That question's still a little off. It's not so much that people are accountable for *not believing in Jesus.* The Bible says we're accountable for *sinning.* There are millions of people who have never heard of Jesus. But they have heard of God. God's first book (creation) is clear to all, such that Scripture warns, "All who sin apart from the law will also perish apart from the law, and all who sin under the law will be judged by the law" (Rom 2:12).

If I've sinned against God, Scripture explains, I'm in bad shape, whether I've heard of Jesus or not. Don't think that sinning against the Father is somehow less serious than sinning against his Son! I know the language sounds harsh to moderns, addicted as we are to sentimental religious books that say only soothing things, but the Bible treats sin, judgment and hell as tragic givens within our present, fallen condition. The Scriptures unapologetically paint a picture of helplessness, guilt and desperate need, such that total disaster can be diverted only if God does something huge.

Our sinful condition takes us back to the beginning, when Adam and Eve first rebelled against their Creator. I've pointed out repeatedly that the world is not what God originally designed it to be. There's a clear break in human history. The delicate perfection of creation shattered upon the stone floor of human sin.

> *When the woman saw that the fruit of the tree was good for food and pleasing to the eye, and also desirable for gaining wisdom, she took some and ate it. She also gave some to her husband, who was with her, and he ate it. Then the eyes of both of them were opened, and they realized they were naked. . . .*
> *So the* LORD *God banished him from the Garden of Eden. (Gen 3:6-7, 23)*

These are the most tragic verses in Scripture. The couple's innocence was lost and their righteousness profaned. The human race lost the Garden, and the ground itself became cursed. From that moment on, there have been no innocent people. Not in Africa. Not in Brooklyn. Nowhere— "for all have sinned and fall short of the glory of God" (Rom 3:23).

I realize that the myth of human goodness remains a powerful one.

But while God's image is still reflected in certain noble qualities even pagans can possess, sin has left a deep mark upon us.

I just leased a new Volkswagen Beetle. I couldn't afford options like a power sunroof or cruise control. I just kept to the standard features like a muffler, headlights, engine—the basics. But I was amazed to learn that included among the standard features was an alarm system. What does it say about the human condition when car alarms are listed as standard equipment?

Indeed, each of us carries in our pockets proof of human sin. Keys. If people weren't prone to steal, doors would not have locks. Our offices could stay unlocked over the weekend. Our cars would still start with a pushbutton. Keys alone are enough to show our guilt.

Each of us tends to think that because I'm not an ax murderer, I'm a good person. I work for a living, pay my taxes and don't usually try to hurt people. But does that make me okay in God's sight? If God made us to be righteous and holy, seeking his glory in all we do, then being decent isn't enough. Even the best of people today fall far, far below the standard God established at creation. And it's a problem of the heart.

Our natures are polluted by sin. We are born guilty and enslaved to sin, without hope unless God has mercy upon us. What is God's perspective on the human condition after the Fall, after corruption?

We'll look at some theological categories like original sin and total depravity. But first we need to realize that the primary biblical insight about God's perspective toward sin is a feeling more than a mental category. God is offended by the human condition. More than that, he is angered by it. The biblical term is *wrathful*. It's not humanity's humanity that angers God. He made our humanity and made it good. What offends our Creator finds is our *in*humanity—the degree to which we fail to be what he designed humanity to be, our corruption, our defilement, our rebellion and our unwillingness to love one another. Yet these inhuman qualities are part of what we are—humanity has become repulsive in the eyes of its Maker. Out of this repulsion comes the Creator's judgment. It's disturbing, but it's also true.

The Marcions Are Coming

Discussing God's wrath today is something of a faux pas. I remember the indignation I felt in eleventh grade American literature when required to read the New England Puritan Jonathan Edwards's sermon "Sinners in the Hands of an Angry God." I was furious over almost every word of this famous biblical oration on hell. I believed in a God of love, after all—who let me do as I please!

Our modern uneasiness with the thought of an angry God is nothing new. One of the earliest of Christian heretics was a man named Marcion. He so hated the concept of a wrathful God that he came up with the notion that there were actually two different Gods in the Bible. One was a peaceful and gracious God—known in our day as the *goduhluv*—the God of the New Testament. The other God was the evil, violent and vengeful God of wrath in the Old Testament. Marcion's great project was to separate the two Gods, so he threw out the Old Testament.

Of course, Marcion also had to get rid of those parts of the New Testament that sounded like the wrathful Old Testament God. When all was said and done, Marcion's Bible only had a few parts of Luke and a couple of Paul's letters left. I guess the problem he had to deal with is the fact that there's a lot of wrath in the New Testament, just as there's a ton of love in the Old Testament.

I wish I could tell you that Marcion's peculiar heresy died with him. But I can't. The churches today are filled with little Marcions. I recently researched contemporary evangelical study Bibles for children and found one that explained that there was a terrible flood in Noah's day, but God wasn't about to let the people die, so he had Noah build an ark.

Did you catch the change? The text of Genesis stresses that God *intended* to kill all of humanity because of its corruption, saving only Noah and his family. This Bible changed the agency for an act of divine judgment from God to natural causes. Sure, I don't like scaring children either, but to change the Bible so that people won't grow up thinking God gets angry is a problem. Is Marcion teaching Sunday school?

We have an inborn tendency to change the face of God, to make him in our image. God knows this weakness, so he reminds us to consider the fullness of his character, his severity along with his love. Both are in the Old Testament, and both are in the New. As Paul commands us in the midst of his great letter of grace: "Consider therefore the kindness *and sternness* of God; sternness to those who fell, but kindness to you, provided that you continue in his kindness" (Rom 11:22, emphasis mine).

Most churches in North America and Europe do a fine job telling people God loves them. But we need also to meditate upon the sternness of God, as he instructs us. And for the next few pages that's what we'll do, keeping in mind that God is not wrathful without reason—it is because of our sin that he is offended. We'll try to stick very close to what the Scriptures actually teach, knowing that we're studying our own *need* for the grace that God freely gives us in Christ—and our need to take the story of Christ to every nation on earth.

We certainly see God's wrath against sinners right off the bat in the Old Testament. The flood by which God killed most of humanity, saving only eight, hits the new Bible reader before he's gotten through the first ten pages (Gen 6—8).

Ponder also the time God burned two young priests—Nadab and Abihu—to death in the temple because they offered sacrifices God hadn't authorized (Lev 10:1-7). It shocks us, but the men had been instructed in how to approach God properly, and they were disregarding that instruction in the very presence of their Lord. Our God is not someone to play games with. He's a consuming fire (Deut 4:24; Heb 12:29). Unless God's grace falls upon us, we are sinners in the hands of an angry God.

Yet God is not capricious. The great creed of the Old Testament says, "The LORD is slow to anger, abounding in love and forgiving sin and rebellion" (Num 14:18). But the very same verse continues, "Yet he does not leave the guilty unpunished; he punishes the children for the sin of the fathers to the third and fourth generation." God is not impulsive or arbitrary, like the explosive, unpredictable parent. His anger is very unlike ours in that it's never motivated by sin but always by righteousness. God's anger is never out of his control. When God brings judgment, it is deliberate, even if it catches us off guard. When we have rebelled against a holy God deserving our infinite obedience, God is always justified in his anger.

The Good Policeman

Remember that it's God's goodness that makes evil so repulsive to him. Consider this story:

> *The Good Policeman was walking down Main Street when he saw a little old lady with a walker crossing the street. As he watched, he saw a large Buick come to a screeching halt next to the little old lady. Three young men hopped out of the car laughing. One of them pushed the old lady to the ground while another started kicking her in the abdomen, the legs and then the face. Even from a distance the Good Policeman could hear bones crack.*
>
> *Finally, one of the young men pulled out a knife, pushed its cold metal against the woman's neck and slit her throat. The Good Policeman witnessed these events. So as the men walked back toward their vehicle, he rushed up to them and thrust his hand out in front of them and said, "Hi. I'm the Good Policeman. And I want you to know that I LOVE you."*

What's wrong with the story? A *good* policeman would have run up to the men, arrested them and taken them to court to be punished. This is not a good policeman but an evil one. If he were good, the guilty would be punished. Yet we expect God to be all love and mercy and grace, with no punishment, no justice, no anger, no wrath. We expect him to see our rebellion and just say, "I love you!" God cannot be good unless he punishes evil.

And God shows his righteous anger in the New Testament every bit as clearly as in the Old. God kills the married couple Ananias and Sapphira for holding back money then lying about it—an event that gripped the church with the fear of God (Acts 5:1-11). God showed his wrath as an act of grace, to purify his church so that it might be holy and devoted as Christ's witnesses to the ends of the earth.

Similarly, God promises judgment on false teachers. Peter uses the coming condemnation of false teachers to encourage his readers (1 Pet 2:1-9). God loves his church and is angered by those who would abuse or harm it. Greedy preachers with false gospels, beware! Our Protector

God can be motivated by both love and anger in defending his bride, the church.

Paul tells the Corinthian Christians that God had taken the lives of some church members because they had been eating the Lord's Supper without loving one another. Paul explains, using sleep as a euphemism for death, "That is why many among you are weak and sick, and a number of you have fallen asleep. But if we judged ourselves, we would not come under judgment" (1 Cor 11:30-31).

And these are just examples of punishments God gives in this life to teach his people to seek his grace. But think about hell for a moment. Did you know that half of the biblical references to the punishments of hell are from the lips of Jesus himself (Mt 5:22, 29; 10:28; 18:9; Mk 9:43-47; Lk 12:5; 16:23)? He described it as a place of eternal fire (Mt 18:8; 25:41) and eternal punishment (Mt 25:46). It's not Ezra who cried, "You snakes! You brood of vipers! How will you escape being condemned to hell?" These are the words of Jesus the Savior (Mt 23:33). Of the condemned sinner we are told:

> *He, too, will drink of the wine of God's fury, which has been poured full strength into the cup of his wrath. He will be tormented with burning sulfur* in the presence of the holy angels and of the Lamb. *And the smoke of their torment rises forever and ever. (Rev 14:10-11, emphasis mine)*

So much for eternal separation from God! There is separation from God's blessedness (2 Thess 1:9). But from another angle, hell is the eternal *presence* of God in unending wrath and judgment. God's anger is not tainted with sin as ours so often is. It's God's prerogative alone to judge. Were I to judge someone as if I were God, it would be sin. I'm just another fallen sinner like everyone else. But God is God, and it's right for him to judge.

Lingering on God's Wrath

I imagine the reason we Christians feel so uncomfortable with God's wrath is because we live in an age of God's patience. Just look at how slow God was to carry out his sentence on Adam. The Lord had told

Adam that he would die when he ate from the forbidden tree (Gen 2:17), but Adam lived 930 years before that death penalty was carried out (Gen 5:5). Only the spiritual alienation from God was immediate—they felt shame (Gen 3:7), hid from God (Gen 3:8), were cursed (Gen 3:16-19) and were expelled from the Garden (Gen 3:23).

But consider Peter's warning about the limitation on God's patience:

> By the same word the present heavens and earth are reserved for fire, being kept for the day of judgment and destruction of ungodly men.
>
> But do not forget this one thing, dear friends: With the Lord a day is like a thousand years, and a thousand years are like a day. The Lord is not slow in keeping his promise, as some understand slowness. He is patient with you, not wanting anyone to perish, but everyone to come to repentance. (2 Pet 3:7-9)

God's patience will come to an end. I imagine it's hard for a physician to tell a terminal cancer patient, "You have three months to live." We shouldn't find it easy to tell a fellow sinner, "God is angry with us and will condemn us without Jesus." But it's the truth.

A Christianity that accentuates the positive without considering the dark side of life in a fallen world fails to fit our experience, let alone Scripture. If God warns of judgment, are we showing kindness when we act like everything's okay? The sin of the prophets and the priests was their crying "Peace, peace!" when there was no peace (Jer 8:11). I'll take one authentic, loving pastor who'll gently but firmly tell me the truth over a thousand who'll tell me what my indwelling sin wants to hear.

As the sociologist James Davison Hunter has documented, evangelical Christians in America today not only want to be *tolerant of* others; we tend to want to be *tolerable to* others.[1] In trying to win the world to Jesus, this is a trap to be avoided. We are not God's public relations advisers.

The problem is that we fail to consider how offensive our sin is to a holy and righteous God. The theme of God's wrath at human sin per-

---

[1]James Davison Hunter, *Evangelicalism: The Coming Generation* (Chicago: University of Chicago Press, 1987), p. 183.

vades Scripture, from Genesis to Revelation. Jesus instructs us to fear one who has the power to throw people into hell (Lk 12:5). This is the fear of one who is utterly holy. Indeed, "The fear of the LORD is the beginning of knowledge" (Prov 1:7). This is a jaw-dropping, heart-stopping fear that shakes us out of our complacency and drives us to seek the merciful face of God in Jesus Christ.

Paul opens Romans—a letter about the gospel's power—with three chapters of guilt and judgment. Paul begins, "The wrath of God is being revealed against all the godlessness and wickedness of men who suppress the truth by their wickedness" (Rom 1:18).

Paul goes on to say God is angry with us because we reject what he tells us in nature (Rom 1:18-23)—strike one against us. We disobey the laws God wrote on our hearts (Rom 1:24—2:16)—strike two. Just think of every time you've criticized someone in your heart. Then imagine all of those judgments being played back to you on judgment day. Could we pass our own standards? Not a chance. And even when God writes everything down for us in Scripture, we use that for religious pride and to judge other people (Rom 2:17—3:8)—strike three. And in God's ballgame it only takes one strike to be out forever. Paul concludes, "There is no one righteous, not even one" (Rom 3:10).

But what if someone really wanted to obey and sought God with all his or her heart? It's never happened. "There is no one who understands, / no one who seeks God" (Rom 3:10-11). The apostle doesn't shield his readers from the consequences of their sin. He drives home the hopelessness of our condition.

Paul understood that until we know we're under God's wrath, we have no need for the gospel of God's grace. It sounds simplistic, but it's the simple truth. Sin explains everything that's wrong in God's good world. How did things get this bad?

Our Declaration of Independence: Original Sin

Why would a good God create a world filled with sin? The short answer: *He didn't.* He created a good world that rebelled against him. Again, we go back to the opening chapters of Scripture.

Adam's sin affected us all. Adam's kids didn't start all over again in the Garden; we all lost our standing with God. This is what we call *original sin*. Adam was our representative as well as our ancestor. His sin was a corporate action under the leadership of the best human being (other than Jesus) who's ever walked the earth—the only one of us that didn't start out with a sinful nature.

We've seen how God places us in a network of authority relationships. Rulers are heads of nations; fathers are heads of families; bosses are heads of companies; Christ, we'll see, is head of the church. When the president and Congress declare war, I'm at war whether I like it or not. If I'm captured by enemy troops, I could object that I never chose even to be an American—it just sort of happened to me when people I didn't elect declared my independence from England back in 1776. I'm really English, I could argue. But they wouldn't buy that. When Thomas Jefferson declared his independence from Britain, he was declaring mine too. He was my head, my representative.

When Adam declared his independence from God, he declared yours and mine. He was our federal head; therefore, his one trespass resulted in condemnation for us all. "Consequently . . . the result of one trespass was condemnation for all men . . . through the disobedience of the one man the many were made sinners" (Rom 5:18-19).

The Christian doctrine of original sin refers not to the *first* sin that Adam and Eve committed in the Garden. Original sin is the resulting guilt that we all bear because our representative Adam rebelled. Some Christians argue that we inherit the propensity to sin, but not the guilt, from Adam. I'm convinced that we inherit both. Guilt is present in every one of us from our conception. Before we ever have a chance to commit a sinful action, we've already failed to measure up to God's perfect standard of righteousness.

Consider how David prayed: "Surely I was sinful at birth, / sinful from the time my mother conceived me" (Ps 51:5). People who are ignorant of God's law still face judgment for Adam's sin. Paul writes, "Nevertheless, death reigned from the time of Adam to the time of Moses, even over those who did not sin by breaking a command, as did Adam" (Rom

5:14). This death comes on account of original sin. Since the Fall we start
out already condemned. We are all original sinners.

Spiritual Corpses: Total Depravity

Being born with the guilt of Adam's sin is enough to alienate us forever
from a righteous and holy God. But as products of the Fall we enter this
world not only guilty but also polluted. To borrow some potentially confusing theological jargon, we enter this world *totally depraved*.

People always ask me about total depravity. It can be a confusing
teaching because it doesn't mean exactly what it sounds like. Total
depravity doesn't mean that people are as bad as they could possibly be.
Rather, total depravity speaks to the effects of the Fall on our totality. Sin
isn't just a problem with wrong thinking. Evil isn't just an emotional
problem. Our irreverence isn't simply seen in our actions. Sin affects our
total persons: our hearts, our heads, our actions, our feelings, our
impulses, our instincts, our tendencies and the whole orientation of our
souls away from God.

Secular academics at times have debated whether evil is caused by
nature or by nurture. Are we born evil, or only become corrupted by bad
environments? Bad environments certainly mold how sin develops within
us—we all learn to follow different idols, but the idolatrous root itself lies
deeper than dysfunctional families and hanging out with the wrong
crowd. Evil originates within the subterranean depths of our souls. Our
families may mold how evil develops in us, but they can't be blamed for
the fact that there is evil within us ready to develop.

We could have the best social services in the universe and still have
corrupt people. Children grow up not only in a sinful world but with sinful hearts in a sinful world. It's not that people are bad because they do
bad things. We do bad things because we're bad people. That's the big
realization God wants us to come to. Until we realize that the problem is
systemic, we won't turn to the root of the problem: the need, not just for
a new rule or a new behavior, but for a new self.

Have you ever fallen into the same sin for the thousandth time and
asked yourself, "How could this happen?" Answer: You were born that

way. There's nothing more wrong with you than with the next guy. It's
not a problem you can fix from the outside in, like that tooth-whitening
system from the drugstore that didn't really work. The problem is at the
root. We're talking about corrupt hearts.

And it's inescapable by human means. Leopards can't change their
spots (Jer 13:23) and dogs return to their vomit (2 Pet 2:22). Adam
handed our free will over to the serpent, so unless the Holy Spirit acts,
we're unable even to believe on our own. We're helpless unless God acts
on our behalf to change us. Notice how Paul explains the way sin affects
our ability to understand the gospel. "The man without the Spirit does
not accept the things that come from the Spirit of God, for they are fool-
ishness to him, and *he cannot understand them*, because they are spiritually discerned" (1 Cor 2:14, emphasis mine). Without the indwelling
Spirit no one is able to believe. The gospel cannot be understood until
after the Spirit is working.

Elsewhere the apostle describes the role Satan plays in keeping
humanity in bondage to unbelief. "The god of this age has blinded the
minds of unbelievers, so that they cannot see the light of the gospel of
the glory of Christ" (2 Cor 4:4). As Martin Luther states in *The Bondage of
the Will,* fallen people are morally incapable of seeking God. The sinner's free will is in bondage to sin because of the Fall.

From conception onward, we human beings are spiritual corpses,
unable to believe and even to cooperate with the Spirit's advances.

The Church's Top Priority

Again, why do we linger on the brokenness of the human condition? The
reason is simple. When we contemplate the terrible reality of being born
defiled and in opposition to a holy God, we're contemplating our soul's
overpowering need for Christ. We're coming face to face with the reason
behind the churches' primary mission: the Great Commission to disciple
the nations (Mt 28:18-20).

The tragedy of sin is the reason for the church's existence as a hospital for sinners, as the beginnings of God's new creation. All of the other
great institutions of this world find their origin in creation—but not the

church. The church is the vanguard of God's new creation, his advance troops carrying the beginnings of new life into all the other spheres of society. What does God require of the churches? A radical commitment to evangelism and global missions. A church without this sense of urgency is dead.

It's sad to admit, but often those of us who have most zealously called Christians to bring God's light to law, medicine, carpentry, the arts and other areas of civilization have been less zealous for Christ's commission to teach the nations. If Christians read my book and somehow think that the Great Commission is less important, then I will have failed.

I have labored to write with a burden that Christians would receive all of life as a gift from God. But I also know there is a danger lurking just around the corner—the danger of taking the gifts of this world and being satisfied to enjoy them ourselves, without exerting every effort to introduce the rest of the world to the Giver of every gift. If you truly love this world God has given us and want to see it restored, it cannot happen without proclaiming Jesus Christ to all the earth. The transformation happens one life at a time, one church at a time.

Global evangelization is God's ordained method for redeeming his creation. While God has revealed himself clearly in creation, the cross of Jesus Christ is not revealed in nature. Hearing this message about Jesus is an essential requirement for saving faith.

Paul emphasizes this necessity in the tenth chapter of Romans. Salvation comes by confessing "Jesus is Lord," he explains, and by believing God raised him from the dead (Rom 10:9). Thus the basic facts of gospel history (like Christ's incarnation and resurrection) need to be understood and received with both mouth and heart (Rom 10:10). And this gospel is the same for every nationality—"Everyone who calls on the name of the Lord will be saved" (Rom 10:13).

But Paul raises a series of rhetorical questions to stress the universal need for evangelization. "How, then, can they call on one they have not believed in?" he asks (Rom 10:14). The implied answer is clear. *They can't*. People have to call on Jesus to be saved, but they can't do that unless they believe in Jesus. And they can't believe in him, he continues, unless they've heard of him. Further, they can't hear of Jesus unless someone preaches to them. And no one will preach to them unless we send them to preach (Rom 10:15). It reads like a geometry proof, but Paul's point is clear: *people won't get right with God until we tell them where to look.*

John Stott observes how Paul's questions "demonstrate the indispensable necessity of evangelism."[2] He writes:

> *The essence of Paul's argument is seen if we put his six verbs in the opposite order: Christ sends heralds; heralds preach; people hear; hearers believe; believers call; and those who call are saved. And the relentless logic of Paul's case for evangelism is felt most forcibly when the stages are stated negatively and each is seen as essential for the next. Thus, unless some people are commissioned for the task, there will be no gospel preachers; unless the gospel is preached, sinners will not hear Christ's message and voice; unless they hear him, they will not believe the truths of his death and resurrection; unless they believe these truths, they will not call on him; and unless they call on his name, they will not be saved.[3]*

Within this passage from Christ's apostle to the Gentiles, Scripture rules out the possibility of reaching salvation through any means other than that of spreading the "word of faith" about Christ. Paul concludes, "faith comes from hearing the message" (Rom 10:17).

No Hope Without Missions

An increasing number of theologians operating within Christian circles today teach that people can be saved without hearing the message. I don't question their sincerity. But sincerity is not the point. The Scriptures know nothing of postmortem evangelism, of a gospel offer beyond the grave for those who didn't hear it in this life. The Bible nowhere teaches us that the Holy Spirit is at work in other religions. Worshiping a God other than Yahweh is idolatry. Approaching the Lord through a

---

[2]John Stott, *Romans* (Downers Grove, Ill.: InterVarsity Press, 1994), p. 285.
[3]Ibid., pp. 286-87.

means other than Jesus Christ is presumption—there is only one way to the Father. And we've seen how the revelation of God in nature shows us only that God is real and that we deserve judgment—the gospel isn't written in the heavens.

The Scriptures consistently work on the assumption that the nations, ours included, are in darkness, and that only the good news about Jesus can bring us to the light. I point this out not to judge other people for their beliefs but to help Christians understand the role they play in supporting brothers and sisters who spread the gospel around the globe.

Even "devout men" such as the Jews at Pentecost (Acts 2:5) are now required to repent and be baptized in the name of Jesus in order to be forgiven of sins (Acts 2:38; 3:19). These are history's most blessed people, having God's covenants, laws and promises. And if God wasn't going to save *them* apart from faith in Jesus, then the rest of us don't stand a chance. C. E. B. Cranfield is right when he comments on Paul's argument in Romans, "If the Jews, the people who might seem to have reason to regard themselves as an exception, are in fact no exception, then without doubt the entire human race lies under God's judgment."[4]

However, seeing the human condition according to God's perspective, while humbling, is not a cause for despair. Rather, it's a call to sober action. There is a gospel, a gospel that is God's power of salvation to all who believe in Jesus Christ, whether Jew or Gentile. Jesus said:

> For God so loved the world that he gave his one and only Son, that whoever believes in him shall not perish but have eternal life. For God did not send his Son into the world to condemn the world, but to save the world through him. Whoever believes in him is not condemned, but whoever does not believe stands condemned already because he has not believed in the name of God's one and only Son. (Jn 3:16-18)

God's word is on the line, and the salvation of millions hangs in the balance. The Lord tells us that those who don't know Jesus need a preacher

---

[4]C. E. B. Cranfield, *Romans: A Shorter Commentary* (Grand Rapids, Mich.: Eerdmans, 1985), p. 67.

sent to them, and he calls us to do the sending. If we dishonor this command in the name of developing a postmodern theology or an inclusive theology or a wide view of God, we will have denied Christ our master.

God Can Do It

The sheer need of the human condition should bind our hearts to seek God in prayer. Sin is stronger than we are. It blinds people to the gospel and leaves them under the power of Satan. This is why Jesus taught us to pray "Deliver us from the evil one" (Mt 6:13). Only God can give people faith. "No one can come to me unless the Father who sent me draws him." But when the Father draws them, Jesus promises, "I will raise him up at the last day" (Jn 6:44).

We can't make people repent. I've tried. It doesn't work. Only God can put repentance in the human heart, and he does it all the time without waiting for us to invite him (Acts 11:18). I don't want to ever hear another sermon about a weakling God helplessly waiting for people to open the doors of their hearts! God busts down the door and announces his arrival with the power of his Holy Spirit. God has the power to remove a heart of stone and replace it with a heart of flesh (Ezek 36:26).

While bringing people the gospel is our job, converting them is God's. He unites dead hearts to Christ and gives them new life (Eph 2:1-5). He breathes on dry bones and resurrects them into a vast army (Ezek 37:9-10). Repentance is a gift of God, not a human work (2 Tim 2:25). God calls us to carry the message and to seek him in prayer, but results are his department.

If God can change the human heart with a single word, then pray big prayers! Don't pray for what you think you can do—that isn't faith. Pray for what you know is impossible. Pray boldly without doubting—it's the Lord who answers (1 Jn 5:14-15). Then start living like it's a done deal. James warns us about half-hearted, mealy-mouthed prayers. "But when he asks, he must not doubt, because he who doubts is like a wave of the sea, blown and tossed by the wind" (Jas 1:6). Prayers that lack boldness are prayers that trust in human power rather than the power of God.

If we're going to see the world according to God, we need to realize that forgiveness is only the beginning of what the Great Commission brings. An honest politician humbles himself as a needy sinner before God. A faithful auto mechanic is one who has Jesus Christ alive within him. A healthy marriage is one where husband and wife both give up their wills and follow God's will instead. As believers are multiplied within each of the spheres of life, each area of civilization is preserved. We are salt, a preservative, and light, diminishing darkness wherever we go (Mt 5:13-14).

If the human condition is as bad as God tells us, then only the Great Commission can restore the cultural mandate. The Great Commission is God's power to bring every sphere of life into obedience to God. Jesus didn't simply commission the church to ask for decisions and count the hands. He calls us to teach the nations to obey everything the Son of God commands, from the cultural mandate in Genesis 1 to the final amen in John's Revelation. This is the church's top priority.

Lord Jesus has total authority over every sphere of life, and he promises that he is with us this very moment. This realization calls for the radical commitment that only comes when we believe the promise that he's inside of us, changing us and his world through us. Here alone is the power to reverse the Fall and renew creation one life at a time.

Then Jesus came to them and said, "All authority in heaven and on earth has been given to me. Therefore go and make disciples of all nations, baptizing them in the name of the Father and of the Son and of the Holy Spirit, and teaching them to obey everything I have commanded you. And surely I am with you always, to the very end of the age." (Mt 28:18-20)

Questions for Discussion

1. You're talking to a friend who objects to the possibility that God could send someone to hell without ever giving that person a chance to hear about Jesus. How might you help this friend understand the situation according to God's perspective?

2. The wrath of God is not God's "dark" side. How is it an expression of God's goodness?

3. What are some reasons we tend to shy away from discussing God's

wrath? Brainstorm some ways you could discuss God's wrath with a person without personally seeming to judge him or her.

4. Explain the difference between the first sin, original sin and total depravity. What impact does it have on you when you consider the state of the human condition?

5. Some Christian teachers say people can go to heaven without the need for evangelism or missions. What biblical passage addresses this? Why is "God's word on the line" in this matter?

6. What is the church's top priority? How does this calling fit with the cultural mandate in Genesis 1 to establish human civilization on the earth?

11

THE COVENANT

Our Relationship with God According to God

"He will crush your head, and you will strike his heel."
GENESIS 3:15

o far we've lingered on the fact that the world and every sphere of life is God's creation. He designed us to civilize the earth; placed us in a network of authority relationships to structure human society (Gen 2:21-24); called us to the holy vocations of work (Gen 2:15), science and education (Gen 2:19-20), sexuality (Gen 1:18; 2:24-25), and communication. God is the trunk from which all the various branches of life spring. Therefore, all of life is a relationship with God.

But we've seen that creation isn't what it once was. At the Fall the world was plunged into sin and despair and so needs the good news that God saves sinners in Christ.

But when we fail to begin in the beginning, we easily miss the awesome scope of the gospel. If we start with Jesus' ministry on earth, then we've skipped over the covenantal context of his ministry. The coming of Christ to earth was merely the central chapter in the unfolding drama of God's saving purpose in history.

If we're going to see God's salvation from his perspective, we take a great step backward to see how things develop. And then what strikes us is that the Bible is a historical account. It's a story, a true story. The main actor is God, and the story is about his fulfilling a promise to his people. This is the big picture that theologians traditionally call the *covenant of grace*.

Sadly, the language of covenants is foreign to most Christians today. A covenant is a legally binding agreement. It's something like a contract, but God's covenants are more unilateral agreements in which God sets all the terms. It's a treaty, with God the sole author. In the ancient Near East, for example, a victorious king would enter into a covenant with a conquered people, promising protection in exchange for loyalty. Such an agreement would carry stipulations—usually tribute—with severe penalties for breaking the covenant, and blessings for obedience. The covenant structured the relationship between the king and that people.

God's Two Covenants: Works and Grace

While there are many smaller covenants in Scripture, God enters into two primary and overarching ones. These present two very different ways of relating to God. God established the first at creation when humanity was still righteous. The other was given after the Fall as a means of reconciliation to God after that righteousness was lost.

At creation God entered into a relationship with the human race. God gave a stipulation: they were forbidden to eat from the tree in the Garden's center. He promised them life upon obedience and death upon disobedience (Gen 2:15-17). Though the term *covenant* is not used in Genesis, it was a structured relationship between God and humanity.

Later, Scripture does use the term *covenant* for this relationship with Adam. Speaking of Israel's turning away from the Lord centuries later, God laments, "Like Adam, they have broken the covenant" (Hos 6:7). This is why many theologians in the Reformed tradition have called this first way of relating to God a *covenant of works*. While the term can be misleading, humanity's continued fellowship with God hinged on our continued obedience to his command.

Apart from Christ, we're all still born within this relationship. God never wiped the slate clean after Adam's sin; the wages of sin remain death (Rom 6:23). In this sense, everyone has a personal relationship with God—*just a bad one, one based on a righteousness they lost.* We're all covenant breakers now, and God owes none of us mercy.

The amazingly good news—in the Old Testament as well as in the New—is that God hasn't left his creation to suffer the death it deserves for breaking this covenant of works. Instead, God has entered into a new covenant grounded solely on his grace. We see this new commitment from God promised in Eden, given to Abraham and his descendents, received by Old Testament Israel, fulfilled in the coming of Jesus Christ and now spreading to all nations by the Holy Spirit's power.

This new commitment God made to a people—a commitment to be their God and to make them his people—has been called by some the *covenant of grace.* This covenant of grace is the difference between hell and heaven, spiritual death and spiritual life. This new relationship, based on God's grace rather than human effort, is the overarching relationship that puts the whole of Scripture into focus.

And the covenant of grace came by God's initiative alone. Though he promised death to Adam and Eve, he nevertheless had mercy upon them. Seeing their shame at their nakedness, he showed them unbelievable love, tenderness and grace, clothing them with garments of skin (Gen 3:21). This new way of relating to God is one in which all the glory goes to him. He gives; we receive.

The Mediator of the Covenant of Grace

Central to this new relationship with God was the establishment of a mediator to intercede between God and his people. When the guy who broke into my Honda and stole my *Saturday Night Fever* soundtrack went to court, I imagine he had a mediator—a court-appointed attorney who pled his case and represented him in a setting where he'd fail on his own. The courtroom gives us a picture of what a mediator does.

When it comes to God and us, God is the offended party, and we're the guilty criminals needing the mediator. We see the mediator of the covenant of grace promised in the very wake of our fall into sin. Right there in Eden, immediately before God laid his curse upon Adam and

Eve, he promised to send a Savior, one of the woman's own descendents, who would defeat the serpent Satan. God cursed the serpent:

> *Because you have done this . . .*
> *I will put enmity*
>   *between you and the woman,*
>   *and between your offspring and hers;*
> *he will crush your head,*
>   *and you will strike his heel. (Gen 3:14-15)*

The woman's offspring, literally her *seed,* refers to future generations. But God isn't talking about all of the woman's descendents but of one descendent in particular. Whenever the Hebrew term *seed* refers to all of one's descendents, it takes a plural personal pronoun *(they)*. But if, as is the case here, it uses the singular personal pronoun *(he)*, it refers to a single individual. Genesis 3:15 *is talking about one man who will defeat Satan.*

And God is referring to Satan—"that ancient serpent" (Rev 12:9)—not to snakes. While he speaks of the woman's seed, he doesn't talk about the serpent's seed but the serpent himself. Right after the Fall, God promises Satan's demise at the hands of a Savior.

We also observe that the serpent will attack the Savior's heel—a serious attack but not usually fatal. The woman's offspring, by contrast, will crush the serpent's head. Crushed heads are fatal.

Sin had only begun to infect the universe when God promised a deliverer, a human being descended from Eve who would conquer Satan and free the world from the grip of the evil one. As Scripture unfolds, we learn that this offspring was Jesus of Nazareth, fully human, but also God in the flesh, the mediator who would succeed where Adam had failed. Jesus Christ is the only mediator in the covenant of grace. "For there is one God and one mediator between God and men, the man Christ Jesus" (1 Tim 2:5).

Christianity is a representative religion—Adam or Christ. There are two covenants: works and grace. Either God deals with us according to our works or according to his grace in Christ. While the normal pattern for us is to enter this life under the covenant of works, God promises to deal with us differently through Christ's covenant. "For as in Adam all die, so in Christ all will be made alive" (1 Cor 15:22).

In Covenant = In Christ, the Covenant Mediator

Have you ever wondered what makes a Christian a Christian? A Roman Catholic would probably say a Christian is a person baptized in the name of the Trinity. A Pentecostal might suggest that a Christian is a believer who's had a powerful experience of the Holy Spirit. Most evangelicals would say that a Christian is a person who trusts in Jesus Christ for salvation. Sometimes we theologians are tempted to think a Christian is someone who knows and accepts sound theology.

While all of these are facets of the Christian life, none of these describes what a Christian actually *is*. They only speak to what a Christian does. The New Testament, like the Old, uses covenantal language to describe what a Christian is. A Christian, the Bible tells us some 164 times in Paul's letters alone, is a person who is *in Christ, in the Lord,* or *in him.*

What does it mean to be *in Christ?* This is covenantal language with an Old Testament precedent; the union with Yahweh that believers enjoyed before the incarnation is spoken of in the New Testament with reference to the mediator of the covenant now revealed: Jesus of Nazareth.

Israel's relationship with God had been compared to a marriage union, binding the "husband" (the Lord) to his "wife" (the people of Abraham; Is 54:5-8). God was a husband to both Israel and Judah (Jer 31:32; see the book of Hosea for a powerful presentation of this image). This relationship between God and his people is pictured the same way in our age: Christ and the church "become one flesh" (Eph 5:31-32). John Calvin could thus exclaim, "We are bone of our Lord Jesus Christ, and . . . we are his flesh."[1] *We are covenantally Christ's bride (Rev 19:7-9).*

Don't think that this is just a metaphor, just Godtalk to express God's love for us. It's one thing to say you love someone; it's something more to give yourself in marriage to someone, which is exactly what God has done to us! And while this union is spiritual, in that we are transformed

---

[1]John Calvin, *Sermons of the Epistle to the Ephesians,* trans. Leslie Rawlinson and S. M. Houghton (Edinburgh: Banner of Truth Trust, 1973), p. 614.

by its power through the Holy Spirit, it is also physical in the sense that it includes our physical bodies in union with Christ's physical human body. God the Son came in the likeness of sinful flesh (Rom 8:3), uniting himself to our fallen human nature and redeeming it in his broken, cursed and resurrected flesh. He is not only a Savior but a brother to us who are his (Heb 2:11, 17). This is a humbling thought.

Jesus is the vine to us, his branches (Jn 15:1-11). From him flows our life and health and "every blessing" in the heavenly realms (Eph 1:3). He is the head to us, his body, to use another biblical image (Eph 4:15-16). He is our covenant mediator; we are united to him in all he has done for us. When he died, we died and were freed from sin's power (Rom 6:3). When he rose, our resurrection to new life became certain (Rom 6:4). We were chosen, accepted, redeemed and predestined in him (Eph 1:4, 6, 7, 11). He sealed us with his Holy Spirit as a sign of our union with him and a guarantee of our salvation's completion at the end of the age (Eph 1:13-14).

When God looks upon his covenanted people, he sees Christ's righteousness and perfection. God's Son stands between the Holy One and us, interceding on our behalf. "Therefore, there is now no condemnation for those who are in Christ Jesus" (Rom 8:1). Blessing for us? "Praise be to the God and Father or our Lord Jesus Christ, who has blessed us . . . with every spiritual blessing in Christ" (Eph 1:3). Even our prayers are offered in Jesus' name—that is, in union with him and through his mediation—such that their answer is certain (Jn 14:14).

How could a sinful creature like me be transformed from the inside out? "Therefore, if anyone is in Christ, he is a new creation, the old has gone, the new has come!" (2 Cor 5:17). Life in covenant with God—in mystical union with Jesus Christ our mediator—is the only source of renewal for a sin-ravaged world. This is the promise stated so simply to our forebears in the Garden.

In the covenant of grace we live by grace. Guilt, shame, fear of hell, and worldly manipulation are not what motivates us to seek the Lord. Truly effective pastors and Christian workers know the Scriptures and trust in God's grace to accomplish God's plan—not in their own human attempts to force the covenant down people's throats.

The Bible as a Covenantal Document

And understanding God's gracious covenant with his people affects how we read the Bible too. Every book of the Bible, without exception, was written for God's covenant people from prophets and apostles and other men who spoke for God to his people. Such a realization impresses itself deeply into our study of the Bible. The biblical books were not addressed to humanity in general.

If every passage of the Bible is covenantal, then every passage assumes a preexisting relationship between God and his people. Every passage of Scripture assumes a context of grace. Are you reading commandments? God did not give them as a means of salvation. God's grace, a saving relationship, was already there. Before God stated the first of the Ten Commandments, he told his people, "I am the LORD your God, who brought you out of Egypt, out of the land of slavery" (Ex 20:2).

These are shocking words. God was saying he actually belonged to this people assembled at Sinai. He was *their* God. Yahweh never said that about any other people on earth. This was a covenantal relationship, a mutual belonging, the reason he rescued his people from the Egyptians. God instructed them to have no other gods, avoid idols, hallow his name, remember his sabbath, honor parents, respect life, keep marriage pure, protect other people's property, speak truthfully and protect their hearts from covetous desire only *after* reminding them of this relationship (Ex 20:3-17).

Understanding the Scriptures as covenantal documents we also realize that every passage points to Jesus Christ, the mediator of the covenant of grace. Jesus rebuked the Pharisees for missing this in their Bible studies. "You diligently study the Scriptures because you think that by them you possess eternal life," he said, "These are the Scriptures that testify about me" (Jn 5:39). All of Scripture is written in the context of a gracious relationship between God and his people—a relationship mediated by God's Son even before he came to earth.

The Gospel Promise of the Covenant of Grace

God's commitment to us, his promises, the gracious and wise instructions we see in his law, our living union with him and the Spirit's power inside us—these sustain us and drive us to seek him day after day. After all, what's ultimately promised in the covenant of grace is not just heaven, forgiveness or joy but God himself, the true prize.

Consider the promise that resonates from Genesis to Revelation. God swears to his people that he will be our God and we will be his people. God's promise to us is not just that we'll know him (Jn 17:3) but more importantly that he'll know us (Jn 10:27).

We see God calling out his people back in Genesis. God chose Abraham, called him away from his own country and people, and gave him the promise that stands for all time upon the sure credibility of God's character.

> *I will make you into a great nation*
> *and I will bless you;*
> *I will make your name great,*
> *and you will be a blessing.*
> *I will bless those who bless you,*
> *and whoever curses you I will curse;*
> *and all the peoples of the earth*
> *will be blessed through you. (Gen 12:2-3)*

The heart of this promise is God's commitment to his people—beginning with Abraham—to be their God and to take them as his own. Even the supposedly new covenant promised through Jeremiah centered on this same promise: "I will be their God, and they will be my people" (Jer 31:33). This promise is unilateral on God's part. When Abraham questioned the promise, the Lord even placed himself under a self-maledictory oath, passing between dismembered animal carcasses (Gen 15:8-18). If the Lord should fail to fulfill his promise—may God be cut in two.

As New Testament believers we've been engrafted into Abraham's covenant. "If you belong to Christ, then you are Abraham's seed, and heirs according to the promise" (Gal 3:29). When history ends and all believers from both testaments stand before the Lord, the same promise will prevail: "'They will be his people, and God himself will be with them and be their God'" (Rev 21:3).

Throughout the Old Testament, God gives a number of specific covenants to his people: the Mosaic law given at Sinai (Ex 19—24), God's promise to lead his people through a descendent of David (2 Sam 7:5-16), the promise of a new covenant for fallen Israel (Jer 31:31-34). Ultimately, however, all of these are administrations of the one overarching covenant of grace promised in Eden and delivered to Abraham (Gal 3:17) and to us.

With the coming of the mediator Jesus Christ, certain aspects of the covenant's administration have changed, so much so that it can even be called a *new* covenant (Heb 7:22). But God's covenant people have always been a people who live by the Lord's promises, not by their own works. Abraham was justified—declared righteous in God's sight—on account of his faith, not by works (Gen 15:6; Rom 4:1-5). David, too, knew that forgiveness for sins was a blessing from God and that his own sins were covered (Ps 32:1-2). It's common for people to say that Old Testament believers were saved by works, but that idea doesn't come from the Old Testament: the whole Bible is a book of grace, a message of blessing grounded on God's promises. This is unconditional grace.

Conditions Within the Unconditional Covenant

Still, God's commandments provide something of a substructure for the covenant of grace, so much so that they are even called the covenant (Deut 4:13). God gives us conditional promises, often by means of his commandments, promising blessing if we trust and obey, and discipline if we disobey. Such conditional promises, however, don't make or break our relationship with God. Rather, they structure it.

When God disciplines us for our sin it is proof that we belong to him. "Endure hardship as discipline; God is treating you as sons. For what son is not disciplined by his father? If you are not disciplined . . . then you are illegitimate children and not true sons" (Heb 12:7-8). God gave Israel the blessings and curses of the Mosaic law (Deut 28). But how often did they return to the Lord only when the curses came for their unbelief? For the people of God, his laws are friends, gracious instructions to keep us walking with him.

This covenantal substructure of laws and conditional promises is just as obvious in the New Testament. God promises that if we humble ourselves

before him, for example, he will lift us up (Jas 4:10). This is a command—
to humble ourselves—coupled with a conditional promise. Similarly, the
command to tithe is instruction coupled with a promise of blessing for
those who obey. Yet these commandments and conditional promises are
all within the context of an unconditional covenant of grace.

But what about these words from Jesus: "I am the vine; you are the
branches. If a man remains in me and I in him, he will bear much fruit;
apart from me you can do nothing" (Jn 15:5)? Does this mean that if we
turn away from Jesus, we lose salvation? That's probably not Jesus' point,
but he does make the promise conditional. To refuse to remain in Christ
is to reject the covenant promise itself that God will be our God and we
his people. Jesus is saying we have to persevere—to keep trusting in
him—in order to continue receiving life from God. In a grace-based relationship with God we continually seek spiritual life from Jesus, who
promises that he will continually give it.

Of course, in saying this he's also stating that he himself is the one
who gives us the strength and heart to persevere. It's ironic that if we do
humble ourselves before God, remain in Christ, believe any promise of
God, it's because God himself has moved our hearts to believe him.
Augustine used to always come back to Paul's question, "What do you
have that you have not received? And if you did receive it, why do you
boast as though you did not?" (1 Cor 4:7). Even obedient faith is a result
of God's grace.

Though there are conditional promises in Scripture, the covenant of
grace is not a conditional covenant. God states it without qualification,
and his powerful purpose assures its realization. Jesus said, "I shall lose
none of all that he has given me" (Jn 6:39). Scripture says that those in
the churches who abandon their faith never had it to begin with—they
were never really numbered among God's people.

Consider John's logic in considering certain people who left Christ in
his day. "They went out from us," he explains, "but they did not really
belong to us." How could John know this? He simply knew that genuine believers do not abandon Christ. He reasons, "For if they had
belonged to us, they would have remained with us; but their going

showed that none of them belonged to us" (1 Jn 2:19).

Central to John's logic is the conviction that authentic ex-Christians don't exist. When God gives grace, you can be confident that "he who began a good work in you will carry it on to completion until the day of Christ Jesus" (Phil 1:6). The covenant of grace is a relationship grounded in a sure promise—not our promise to God but God's promise to us. His discipline serves only to keep us dependent on him for grace.

The People of the Covenant of Grace

Often we're tempted to think of salvation as a strictly personal affair. Certainly God calls each and every Christian individually to faith and new life in Christ, but in so doing he's numbering us among his covenant people. We aren't the persons of God but the people of God. We live in union with other people, under the authority of others and with our destinies tied to theirs. As God's image we were created as relational beings, reflecting the community within God himself.

We should therefore expect that, when God redeems us, he's not going to leave us alone as individuals but will instead incorporate us into a community. This people of God was composed of believing Israel before Christ's coming, and now includes both Jews and Gentiles who turn to Jesus (Eph 3:6). He calls his people his church (Mt 16:18), his bride (Rev 19:7), his dwelling (Eph 2:22), God's household and the church of the living God (1 Tim 3:15). The church is the family of God (1 Pet 4:17), his flock (1 Pet 5:2), his temple (Eph 2:21), the city of God (Rev 3:12), and the pillar and foundation of the truth (1 Tim 3:15).

Just like Israel had been a chosen people (Is 65:9), a royal priesthood (or kingdom of priests) and a holy nation (Ex 19:6) that belonged to God (Lev 25:55), so now is the church: "But you are a chosen people, a royal priesthood, a holy nation, a people belonging to God" (1 Pet 2:9). The church is the very Israel of God (Gal 6:16).

I've known a lot of Christian lone rangers. They tend to be prone to heresies and are frequently enslaved to sins like anger, judgmentalism, divisiveness and bitterness. Evidently Augustine knew the type, arguing the absurdity of claiming God as your Father without accepting the church as your mother. Tertullian stated that outside the church there is no salvation—a conviction affirmed again and again throughout history by Protestants every bit as much as Catholics.

It's not that people can't encounter Jesus and his salvation unless they're church members. But when God saves people, he places them into a community of fellow believers who encourage them, pray for them, serve them and are served by them, correct as necessary and train them. Scripture says we are one body with many parts, Christ being the head. None of these parts can exist on its own, the whole needing every member (1 Cor 12:12-31).

In the description of the early church, the believers' commitment to one another stands out. While they devoted themselves to the apostles' teaching, the Lord's Supper and prayer, they also "devoted themselves to . . . the fellowship" (Acts 2:42). They were "together" (Acts 2:44), sacrificing greatly for each other. They continued to meet "together" and broke bread "together" (Acts 2:46).

A great many biblical passages tell us to commit ourselves to other believers, to the church, and even to submit to and obey the elders of a specific church (Heb 13:17). God's grace works in us among his covenant people as we look to Scripture together, pray together, devote ourselves to one another and take the Lord's Supper together. The church is an organism, a single people covenanted to God forever through his mediator Jesus Christ.

The Optimism of the Mustard Seed

Just like God's covenant grew outward from Israel to take in Gentiles—non-Jews—in Judea, Samaria, Asia, Greece and Rome, so it continues to grow at an accelerated rate even as you're reading this.

I realize that the Christian bestseller list is usually filled with books promising that this world is getting worse and worse. Is the world filled with evil? Of course. That's why we need a gospel. Have the moral standards of Western culture declined in recent decades? You bet. But the kingdom of God is not limited to the moral standards of fickle Americans. Even if America should falter, God stands by his covenant promise.

If we take a break from examining our proverbial trees, what kind of forest is out there? What is Jesus Christ doing on planet earth right now? When I turn my ears away from the doom-and-gloom discouragers, I'm astounded by the sheer numbers of people committing their lives to Jesus Christ. In A.D. 30 only a handful were following Jesus. Yet God took a few men and women and, building on the covenant promises given to his people and fulfilled in Christ, turned the world upside down.

Of course, worlds don't turn over overnight. According to estimates from the U.S. Center for World Mission, it took until about 1430 just to reach the 1 percent milestone—one in a hundred people were biblical Christians. I'm not sure how they came up with the estimates, but the numbers are staggering. It took another three and half centuries to double the percentage of the world's population that knew Jesus Christ—to about 2 percent by 1790. Since then, God's covenant people have seen exponential growth:

3 percent by 1940
4 percent by 1960
5 percent by 1970
6 percent by 1980
7 percent by 1983
8 percent by 1986
9 percent by 1989
10 percent by 1993
11 percent by 1997[2]

I remember hearing one secular historian observe that the growth of biblical Christianity has been *the* religious story of the past fifty years. Even if these numbers are only half right, we are living in the greatest revival in Christian history.

Today almost half the population of South Korea—once a Buddhist nation—claims to be Christian. There are more Presbyterians in Korea

---

[2]You can access missions-related statistics online at <www.missionfrontiers.org>. *Mission Frontiers* is a publication of the U.S. Center for World Mission.

than in America. Korea is now sending over three thousand missionaries to other parts of the world so that people in places like America can know Jesus too.

Look at Latin America. In Chile, once home to the deadest Catholicism, one third of the people now affiliate with Bible-believing Protestant churches. Or consider Brazil. By 1990 there were 7,466 Catholic churches, and 60 percent of the people were involved in occult practices. But God had been doing something big. By that same year there were 148,976 Protestant churches, and most of them gospel-centered and Bible-based. About one in five Brazilians today claims to be a born-again, evangelical Christian.

But the hot spot for the gospel right now is Africa. Over a third of the people of Kenya have placed their faith in Jesus Christ. In Uganda one person in four professes saving faith in Jesus, despite years of political turbulence. Indeed, it was Zambia—not the United States—that declared itself a Christian nation in the 1990s. The president of Zambia declared his country a "Christian nation" and prayed a prayer of repentance on behalf of the people, confessing specific sins like idolatry and pleading for the blood of Jesus to cover them.

We may not have been listening, but Jesus told us his kingdom would grow. He explained that God's rule on earth would be like a mustard seed that began tiny but grew huge (Mt 13:31-32). God's kingdom would work through all the nations like yeast through dough (Mt 13:33). God's covenant blessings have invaded this earth and are expanding rapidly.

This was the picture the prophets gave centuries before Christ came. Isaiah was given a vision of the *last days*—a term used in the New Testament not in reference to the last few years before the second coming but to the entire Messianic era, the age between Christ's two comings, that being *right now* (Acts 2:17; 1 Tim 4:1; Heb 1:2). In this age, "The mountain of the LORD's temple will be established as chief among the mountains . . . and all the nations will stream to it" (Is 2:2). "Many peoples"— not just the Jews—"will come and say, / 'Come, let us go up to the mountain of the LORD. . . . He will teach us his ways, / so that we may walk in his paths'" (Is 2:3). This is imagery—geographical changes aren't the point. Rather, many peoples will worship the God of the Jews.

Despite constant counterattacks from the evil one, this age is increasingly coming to look the way Habakkuk foresaw it: "The earth will be filled with the knowledge of the glory of the LORD / as the waters cover the sea" (Hab 2:14). I don't know how much of this will be accomplished before the Lord returns. We may be drawing near to the end, or it could still be a long way off. It could be that fifty thousand years from now church history books will cover our era under the heading "Part One: The Early Church."

Whenever the Lord returns, I'm confident that God stands by his promises. His people will be a great multitude from every nation (Rev 7:9-10) and will be the light not only of Israel but of the whole earth (Mt 5:14). When we get the big picture of God's relationship with us, we're given eyes to see that King Jesus truly is taking back his earth.

Questions for Discussion

1. What was the first covenant God made with humanity? Is it still in force? What implications might it carry for your Christian ministry?

2. In your own words, what is the covenant of grace? How does it give you the big picture of salvation? Where is the covenant of grace promised?

3. What is a mediator? What difference does it make to know that God has given us a mediator in Jesus?

4. What New Testament phrase best describes our being in covenant with God through his appointed mediator? How is it significant to your Christian life?

5. What did God promise to Abraham? How is that promise carried throughout the rest of the Bible?

6. In what ways are the Old and New Testaments the same? How do they differ? Critique the statement "Old Testament believers were saved by their good works."

7. A young Christian tells you he doesn't need church since he's got Jesus. What might you say to him?

8. Is the biblical vision for God's work in this age optimistic or pessimistic? Discuss what God is doing on earth today.

12

THE SHIP
WILL RISE AGAIN

Suffering, Death and the Life Beyond According to God

"For dust you are,
and to dust you will return."
GENESIS 3:19

We opened with a quote from a popular Bible teacher who asked why waste our time polishing the brass of this world if the ship itself is sinking. By looking back to God's design, we saw that God made us to pilot the ship of this world—and to polish the brass. It's what we were made for as human beings. Still, that Bible teacher was right about one thing: the ship is definitely sinking. We live in a dying world filled with suffering.

After the Fall, God cursed the earth itself, telling Adam, "Cursed is the ground because of you" (Gen 3:17). Pain entered into the life of both man and woman, suffering that would culminate in death.

"By the sweat of your brow
you will eat of your food
until you return to the ground,
since from it you were taken;
for dust you are
and to dust you will return." (Gen 3:19)

But what does our suffering mean?

For those outside the covenant of grace, the suffering of this world is an urgent warning to turn to God. When the tower in Siloam collapsed and killed eighteen people, people wondered if God killed them because they were worse sinners than the rest of us. Jesus said these victims were no guiltier than anyone else. "But unless you repent, you too will all perish" (Lk 13:5). Jesus didn't correct his hearers for assuming that God took these people's lives. Jesus corrected them for thinking *they themselves deserved better* from God. His response was the same when questioned about some Galileans who suffered (Lk 13:3). Suffering is a sober warning. Judgment awaits us unless we turn to Jesus Christ in repentance.

It's a powerful warning and should even give believers pause. Christians, though forgiven of both Adam's guilt and their own, nevertheless must pass through suffering and death. The same Lord who calls us into his covenant as our God also calls us to suffer and die.

What God's Doing When Christians Suffer

It's tempting to say that bad things happen to us just because we live in a fallen world full of sin and its consequences, but God tells us much more. God isn't concerned to vindicate his involvement in our suffering. He says he's the one bringing us pain, beginning with the curse he laid on us in Eden. But we can always be certain that God has a purpose in our suffering. When you suffer as a believer, your pain is united to Jesus who suffered, and his purpose overrules it all. What is God's purpose when we suffer?

Suffering glorifies God. Many Christians assume God is trying to teach us some lesson in our suffering, which is often the case. But not always. Think of Job. God wasn't trying to teach Job anything. He wasn't punishing or disciplining Job. God was winning a wager against Satan, proving that the Lord is worthy of praise whether he brings prosperity or pain. But God wasn't arbitrary in this—he was silencing his critics, putting the Evil One to shame, and bringing honor to his own holy name (Job 1:6-12). Even when God didn't tell Job why, he infused Job's suffering with incredible significance.

No one enjoys suffering, but we need to examine our priorities if we're unwilling to suffer for the glory of God. We saw in chapter two that God refuses to share his glory with anyone (Is 48:11). He made us, and he can do with us as he pleases. We exist for his glory, not our own.

When all is said and done, the hard experience you walk through may be more about God's purposes than about you and your sin. Your boss tells you your position has been terminated, your child is struck by a drunk driver, or your doctor tells you it's cancer. What's going on? God may not show you this side of death, but you can know that such terrible experiences may not be mainly about you at all. He may be putting his glory on display before the angels by bringing you faithfully through trials.

Suffering disciplines us. While Job's suffering was not on account of his sin, sometimes God uses suffering to call us to himself. Sometimes God brings us suffering because we've sinned, and he's disciplining us. The Israelites learned again and again about God's disciplinary love. The cycle throughout the book of Judges, for example, is that God's people turn away from him, and he sends evil. Only after great suffering do they call out to God in repentance, so that God raises up a judge to liberate them.

On a more personal scale, it's like parenting—only we're the kids. Like stubborn little children, we demand our own way. Many have observed that we're more likely to call out to God during times of trouble. What we fail to realize is that God may be bringing us the trouble in the first place so we'll do precisely that.

We're sinners, and the penalty for sin is death. The simple fact that we don't suffer more is itself evidence of God's mercy. And the fact that he uses suffering for a redemptive purpose—teaching us to seek him—is an incredible example of God's triumph over evil.

Remember when the Israelites complained about their food? God had miraculously given them manna to eat day after day for years, but they grew tired of the monotony, saying, "We detest this miserable food!" (Num 21:5). As a consequence, God sent venomous snakes among them, killing many. But God didn't simply send snakes to punish the people.

He brought the people to repentance, and they confessed their sin.

What God did next amazes me. He told Moses to create a snake out of bronze and stick it on a pole. Like us, the Israelites were too sinful to be able to approach God directly, so the snake served as a mediator, a symbolic go-between. Whenever an Israelite looked to the bronze snake—God's mediator—he or she lived (Num 21:7-9).

Jesus referred to this experience in the third chapter of John's Gospel. A lot of Christians have memorized John 3:16, the famous verse about God so loving the world, but the context of this remark was a discussion of the bronze snake from Numbers. Jesus said:

> *Just as Moses lifted up the snake in the desert, so the Son of Man must be lifted up, that everyone who believes in him shall have eternal life.*
>
> *For God so loved the world that he gave his one and only Son, that whoever believes in him shall not perish but have eternal life. (Jn 3:14-16)*

The bronze serpent was a type of Christ, a symbol of the coming messiah, Jesus, our covenant mediator. God was teaching his people to look to God through a mediator. His punishment for believers always has this same redemptive purpose. He's turning us to Jesus, teaching us, changing us, molding us into the sons and daughter he's made us to be.

There are times when God takes a hammer and smashes us into a thousand pieces. It's easy to think then that God must hate us, but actually it's his love that does it. God never stops with punishment with his loved ones. The Bible tells us to consider it joy when we face trials because they make us complete (Jas 1:2-4). He destroys us only so he can refashion us. He breaks us only so he can fix us properly. When bad things happen to us, God makes us whole.

Suffering trains us for future battles. Even when we haven't done anything particularly wrong, God brings suffering to train us in Christian living. Peter tells us that trials come "so that your faith—of greater worth than gold, which perishes though refined by fire—may be proved genuine and may result in praise, glory and honor when Jesus Christ is revealed" (1 Pet 1:7).

As a goldsmith refines gold, our reliance on Jesus Christ (which is far more eternal than gold) is refined by grief. Think of all the impurities God burns away in the fires of affliction—self-reliance, unwillingness to accept change, the prideful assumption we can handle things on our own. As the Lord burns these away, our faith becomes stronger and more visible. I remember one Christian man who had struggled with cancer for many years. Though he'd served the Lord for decades, he exclaimed, "I didn't even begin to live until I got cancer!"

Suffering helps us receive grace. Sometimes God brings pain into our lives to help us rely more on his grace. Consider Paul's thorn in the flesh. Christians don't know exactly what the thorn was: a particular sin that Paul couldn't be freed of? An illness or some spiritual attack? Whatever evil it was, God refused to take it away. Paul tells us why:

> *To keep me from becoming conceited because of these surpassingly great revelations, there was given me a thorn in my flesh, a messenger of Satan, to torment me. Three times I pleaded with the Lord to take it away from me. But he said to me, "My grace is sufficient for you, for my power is made perfect in weakness." Therefore I will boast all the more gladly about my weakness, so that Christ's power may rest on me. (2 Cor 12:7-9)*

Obviously the suffering Paul experienced—he calls it torment—was an evil thing in it's own right—a messenger of Satan. But God is also the one who gave the torment in order to keep Paul from becoming arrogant. Paul's thorn drove him to his knees, teaching him to live by God's grace alone. Paul's weakness gave Jesus an opportunity to display his power.

God may not show us what he's doing behind the scenes, but we can know our suffering takes on significance beyond the simple fact that the world is under the curse. We suffer in union with the one who suffered for us. We suffer in Christ, with Christ, through Christ and for Christ, so that his purpose might come to fruition and he might receive glory, honor and praise. That's enough. His grace is sufficient for me, and it's enough for you too.

Suffering also reminds us that human life is 100 percent fatal. It's only the dead in Christ who have reached the land of the living. This world is disintegrating, and our days are numbered. Pain is a call to live spiritually Spartan lives filled with grace but nothing more, lives that hear how quickly death is approaching.

Five Myths About Death

Death is the climax of the life of suffering. But there's a lot of confusion about it these days. Let's consider five popular myths.

1. We shouldn't talk about death. Society has become very good at denying the reality of death. On the one hand, we're seeing more death than ever before. We see scores of fictional deaths on television every night—deaths as fake as George Washington's teeth. It's like video-game death.

The irony is that, with all the violence on television, people rarely talk about dying. Think of all the euphemisms we use to avoid mention of death. Next time you're having dinner with a friend, try asking if he or she ever thinks about dying. As an experience that you and I will both go through, talk of death is taboo. But the Bible gives over a thousand references to death and dying.

2. Death due to natural causes. You might think it odd to call "natural" death a myth, but death is not natural for human beings. It is an enemy (1 Cor 15:26), an invader within God's good creation (Rom 5:12). Death is the unnatural separation of body and soul, the ripping apart of two realities God designed for unity. Death is an evil, a desecration and a curse—yes, a just curse given by God—but a curse of the Fall, nonetheless (Gen 3:17-19).

Think of how Jesus responded when his friend Lazarus died. Jesus wept over Lazarus (Jn 11:35). Why? It wasn't because the situation was hopeless—Jesus raised his friend from death just moments later. Nor was it because Jesus missed him—again, he took care of that. Jesus wept because his friend had succumbed to something evil. An enemy. God's heart is opposed to death, and so should our hearts be.

3. God has nothing to do with death. God hates death. He weeps over Lazarus but takes no pleasure in the death of the wicked either (Ezek 18:23). But let us not naively think that he has nothing to do with death.

Scripture is so direct: "There is no god besides me," the Lord says. "I put to death and I bring to life" (Deut 32:39). Again, "The LORD brings death and makes alive; / he brings down to the grave and raises up" (1 Sam 2:6). Even when animals die, Scripture teaches, it's because God actively takes away their breath (Ps 104:29). God is sovereign over life and death, and when death comes your way, it won't be because the devil won and God lost or because you just didn't have enough faith to live any longer.

I heard a mother recently who had lost her teenage son in a drug-related shooting sob, "If this was my will, it wouldn't be this way. But this was God's will. So I accept it." Some might criticize her for not dealing with the reality of her loss, but I think she shows a depth of faith I need in my own life. The Grim Reaper doesn't hold the keys of death; Jesus Christ does (Rev 1:18).

Does this mean we shouldn't try to extend our lives through medicine and healthy living? Of course not. God also reminds us that we're responsible for our actions. The Jewish king Hezekiah lived an extra fifteen years, for example, because God heard him pray (Is 38:5). And if death is an enemy, we should oppose it. Even Jesus was overwhelmed by sorrow at the thought of dying, and he prayed to the Father asking to avoid it—though he was willing to face it if there was no other way to save us (Mt 26:36-42). And face it he did. When we look to Jesus not only as our Savior but also our example, we know it is right to fight the approaching death, so long as we are willing—like Jesus—to face whatever we must for God's purpose.

4. Death before one's time. Have you ever worried about the timing of death? Will I leave children with no one to care for them? Will I pass away before I could have led my cousin to faith in Christ? I can't answer all these questions, but I think Scripture reassures us that God will not let us die until the exact moment he has prepared.

God doesn't just bring death in some general sense; he oversees the exact moment each of us will pass from this earth.

Man's days are determined;
> *you have decreed the number of his months*
> *and have set limits he cannot exceed. (Job 14:5)*

Job was saying that God is in charge even of the hour of our passing. There is a time to die, Scripture tells us (Eccles 3:2). Paul told the philosophers in Athens that God determines the times set for people (Acts 17:26). It was God who said to the rich man, "You fool! This very night your life will be demanded of you" (Lk 12:20). God's hand is at work in everything that happens. If God works all things together for the good of those who love him (Rom 8:28), then surely the hour of our death is not overlooked.

5. *Death is final.* One of the great differences between grieving over the death of a Christian and the death of an unbeliever flows from the realization that death is not final. The believer grieves over a fellow Christian's death—just like Jesus grieved over Lazarus—but does not grieve with despair like a non-Christian does. "Brothers, we do not want you to be ignorant about those who fall asleep, or to grieve like the rest of men, who have no hope" (1 Thess 4:13). Christ died and rose and is returning. Jesus has "destroyed death and has brought life and immortality to light through the gospel" (2 Tim 1:10). For the Christian, death is a transition, an end to a life of suffering, and a beginning of a freedom we now only taste in part.

Preparing for Death

Since death is a reality each of us will face, how can we prepare for it? The Lord tells us not to fear dying—Jesus died to free us from the fear of death (Heb 2:14-15). His most common command during his ministry was "Don't be afraid" (see, for example, Mt 10:31; 14:27; 17:7; 28:10).

The process of dying brings to its victims a profound sense of loss that can tempt one to despair or be an opportunity to grow ever closer to our God. The dying process makes satisfaction in our circumstances more difficult, so that the only choice remaining is either to delight in God alone or not delight at all. It's no surprise that bitterness is the secret sin of many sick and elderly people. The inevitability of death for every one of us is an occasion to test our soul's aliveness to God.

The flipside of being alive to God is being dead to sin. When Jesus told his followers to take up their cross, he wasn't talking about jewelry

(Mk 8:34). The call to discipleship in Jesus is a call to die on a regular basis. "I die every day," Paul exclaims (1 Cor 15:31). To die to sin is to give up your preferences, interests and needs in order to look to God for grace and truth and life. For the Christian, physical death brings freedom from this struggle. He who has died daily finds it easier to die one last time.

Tragically, by contrast, there is no silver lining in death for the unbeliever. To die in unbelief is to die under the wrath of God, without any hope for salvation. Scripture testifies: "Man is destined to die once, and after that to face judgment" (Heb 9:27).

I've been asked on many occasions about those who die in infancy. I honestly don't know how to answer this question. If we stick close to what the Bible actually teaches, we're left with only a partial answer. Scripture is clear that no fallen human being, no matter how young, is righteous enough to deserve eternal life—sinners are sinners even from the womb (Ps 58:3). Still, Scripture tells us that children of believers are treated differently from others. If even one parent believes, Paul tells us, their children are holy to God (1 Cor 7:14). It seems that one of the benefits of life in Christ is the spiritual blessing of the covenant of grace on your children. I can assure grieving Christian parents that their children receive blessing in God's presence.

But what about the children of unbelievers? Scripture gives no universal promise of salvation to children just because they are young, but neither does it speak explicitly about children being sent to hell. Augustine proposed limbo: sort of the best room in hell, one without pain but equally without blessing. That was speculation. Others have suggested that God unites them to Christ upon their deaths. But that's equally speculative. When I look at the Bible alone, all I can say is that such children are sent into the hands of a just and loving God. But that's all I can say. I'm deeply concerned about the fate of children outside Christ; I'm not convinced that Americans are sending the million-and-a-half babies they abort each year to heaven. Such children are sent before eternal judgment as fallen sinners without Christ. The picture looks bleak, but Scripture simply doesn't tell us for sure. Their fate remains a mystery.

Certainly if children in unbelieving homes are sent away from God's presence because they are fallen, it sheds new light on how deeply wrong it is when parents turn from God. Parents forfeit not only their own souls but also the souls of their children. Such a terrifying possibility should make Christians even more committed to bringing the good news of Christ to all people, no matter their age.

I know this partial answer will satisfy practically no one, but it's the best I can do—and I am suspicious of those who think they have more of an answer. We do well to be silent where Scripture is silent. "The secret things belong to the LORD our God, but the things revealed belong to us and to our children forever, that we may follow all the words of this law" (Deut 29:29). The fate of children outside Christian homes is a secret thing of God, but what is clearly revealed is how we can prepare for death here and now:

> *Repent and be baptized, every one of you, in the name of Jesus Christ for the forgiveness of your sins. And you will receive the gift of the Holy Spirit. The promise is for you and your children, and for all who are far off—for all whom the Lord our God will call. (Acts 2:38-39)*

The Ship Will Rise Again

Because our sins are forgiven through Jesus Christ, the Christian's death is not final. We should, however, consider what awaits us beyond the grave. The biblical picture is quite different from the image in cartoons. God doesn't intend me to stand around on a cloud all day with a harp. And God certainly isn't going to turn us into angels—that's an entirely different species!

We don't have a lot of details, but Scripture lays out the basic plan for life beyond the grave. The point to which God directs our attention is our bodily resurrection from the grave at the second coming of Jesus Christ.

Jesus' return is a pervasive cause for hope within the New Testament. Jesus taught us that he would return in the Father's glory, accompanied by angels (Mt 16:27). Elsewhere, he said that he would come in his own glory, accompanied by angels (Mt 25:31).

Paul calls us to eagerly await or long for Christ's second coming

(1 Cor 1:7; 2 Tim 4:8). Hebrews reassures us that Christ will come "a second time" to bring his salvation to those who are waiting for him (Heb 9:28). Peter reminds us that the Lord will come like a thief (2 Pet 3:10). John tells us that when Christ returns, we'll be like him because we'll see him as he actually is (1 Jn 3:2). John concludes his apocalypse with prayer for Jesus to return (Rev 22:20).

Christ's return is our cause for hope because he's coming back to finish the job he started thousands of years ago. When God promised to crush the serpent back in Genesis 3:15, he set in motion the expectation that he'd repair our sin-damaged world. When Jesus came, he purchased the redemption he'd begun through his promises to Israel, and when he left, he did so with the further promise to return (Acts 1:11). When he does come back, he's going to complete the world's salvation.

The biblical vision for the age to come has nothing to do with clouds. Indeed, it's a very physical vision, a corporeal vision. On the last day, when Christ returns to earth in glory, *we're going to get our bodies back.* "For the Lord himself will come down from heaven, with a loud command, with the voice of the archangel and with the trumpet call of God, and the dead in Christ will rise first" (1 Thess 4:16). God created the human person as a unity of body and soul, and that unity will be restored.

For believers still alive on earth at Christ's return, their bodies will be transformed miraculously without ever passing through death (1 Thess 4:17). For the rest of us, there's resurrection. Either way, we all get new bodies. Jesus—who experienced the only true resurrection so far—is the prototype. Other resurrections—like Lazarus—were only temporary resuscitations. They went on to die again, but we'll all be raised permanently when Jesus comes back.

> But our citizenship is in heaven. And we eagerly await a Savior from there, the Lord Jesus Christ, who, by the power that enables him to bring everything under his control, will transform our lowly bodies so that they will be like his glorious body. (Phil 3:20-21)

Our new bodies won't be exactly like our current bodies: we won't have love handles or double chins, and we'll have perfectly flat washboard abs . . . Strike that. I can't back it up with Scripture. Still, there *will* be a difference.

While our current bodies are perishable because of the Fall, our new bodies will never die (1 Cor 15:42). And whereas our current bodies are dishonorable—pus, bile, phlegm, fat, sweat, urine, that crusty stuff in your eyes—our resurrected bodies will be honorable. While the bodies we have now are weak, they'll become powerful when Jesus comes back (1 Cor 15:43). And if our bodies now are fitted to fallen nature, they'll become perfectly fitted to the life of the Holy Spirit (1 Cor 15:44).

But our resurrection bodies will still be *physical* bodies. After his resurrection Jesus ate food (Lk 24:41-43). He could be touched (Jn 20:27). "Look at my hands and feet. It is I myself! Touch me and see; a ghost does not have flesh and bones, as you see I have" (Lk 24:39). Our resurrected bodies will be recognizable, as Jesus was (Jn 20:16), and the marks from his wounds were still visible (Jn 20:20).

Until that time, believers who die are with the Lord in heaven. We won't be unconscious during this intermediate state. Jesus told the thief on the next cross, "I tell you the truth, today you will be with me in paradise" (Lk 23:43). Paul said to die was to "be with Christ" (Phil 1:23). And to be away from the body is to be "at home with the Lord" (2 Cor 5:6, 8). I suspect we'll be visible and recognizable, as were Elijah and Moses when they appeared during Christ's transfiguration (Mt 17:3). But I'm not sure how this all works, since we won't have the bodies left in the grave, nor have our resurrection bodies yet. As I've said before, doing theology is like putting a puzzle together with half the pieces missing. We'll have to wait until we die to find out all the details.

Our resurrection from death is in preparation for God's final judgment, when all the nations will be resurrected—unbelievers as well (Dan 12:2). Jesus will separate us into two groups: his sheep to his right, the rest—goats—to his left (Mt 25:31-46). "They will go away to eternal punishment," Jesus explains, "but the righteous to eternal life" (Mt 25:46).

While we're reconciled to God—justified—by faith alone apart from works (Rom 3:22, 28), our judgment at history's end will be according to our works (2 Cor 5:10). This confuses a lot of people. The solution is the

fact that when Christ saves a person, he begins changing them. The same
Spirit who gives us saving faith (Eph 2:1-10) also bears his fruit in our
lives—love, joy, peace, patience, kindness, goodness, faithfulness, gen-
tleness and self-control (Gal 5:22-23).

The same Lord Jesus to whom we're united by faith develops in us a
Christlike character. You "work out your salvation with fear and trem-
bling," but it's really "God who works in you to will and to act according
to his good purpose" (Phil 2:12). When we stand before Christ on the last
day, our sins will have been removed from us (Ps 103:12), and only the
Spirit's fruit in us will remain. Even the righteous works that set us apart
from others will ultimately be God's doing and not our own, so that all
the glory goes to him.

Eternally Polished Brass

Heaven isn't the final destination of those who know God. Heaven is
only a temporary holding area until the resurrection and the renewal of
the earth. Christ's return—the "day of the Lord"—will not only bring
judgment but the complete renewal of God's created order, a cosmic salvation.

> *That day will bring about the destruction of the heavens by fire, and the ele-*
> *ments will melt in the heat. But in keeping with his promise we are looking*
> *forward to a new heaven and a new earth, the home of righteousness. (2 Pet*
> *3:12-14)*

John's revelation also pictures "a new heaven and a new earth" following the last judgment (Rev 21:1). This is not newness in time or origin
but newness of nature or quality.[1] In other words, we'll live on a
renewed earth.

John describes for us the final coming together of heaven and earth.
The Holy City comes down from heaven (Rev 21:2) and God sets up his
home right here on earth (Rev 21:3)—just like he walked with Adam in

---

[1]See Anthony Hoekema's discussion in *The Bible and the Future* (Grand Rapids, Mich.:
Eerdmans, 1979), p. 280.

the Garden. Scripture reveals an amazing mystery. *We aren't going to heaven. Heaven is coming to us.* We're going to enjoy heaven on earth.

God's not going to annihilate his favorite planet. When Jesus said the meek would inherit the earth, he wasn't promising them a heap of ashes (Mt 5:5). Of course, if they really were meek, they'd be content with ashes, but that's not the point. The earth will pass through the fires of judgment, but the world that arises like a phoenix from the ashes will be a renewed version of the earth we live on now.

The creation waits in eager expectation for the sons of God to be revealed. For the creation was subjected to frustration, not by its own choice, but by the will of the one who subjected it, in hope that the creation itself will be liberated from its bondage to decay and brought into the glorious freedom of the children of God. (Rom 8:19-21)

The world, according to God, is not temporary. Christ is going to free it, not kill it. God made it to last and last it will. His redeeming love will restore the entire cosmos to the glory it had in the beginning. We'll return again to the Eden God designed, though it will have developed into a great city (Rev 21:16, 22). The apostles can even speak of the return of Christ as "the time . . . for God to restore everything" (Acts 3:21). God's world was broken, but when Jesus returns, he's going to fix it.

And don't assume the life to come will be a never-ending hymn sing. God's going to be the center of attention, but the biblical descriptions aren't just of worship. We'll live in a city, and we'll probably eat. Jesus described the coming age as a feast that people travel to from east and west (Mt 8:11). Isaiah describes the new heaven and new earth as one in which people from every part of the globe come to worship and serve God in Jerusalem (Is 66:19-24). I suspect we'll work in our God-given callings, walk through fields, live in houses and do all the things God designed us to do in the beginning. People often think I'm joking, but I'm dead serious when I say I want to be an architect on the new earth.

Revelation pictures all the nations coming before God and presenting him with their "glories" (Rev 21:26). Picture each nationality's treasures— palaces, artwork, cuisine, drama, music, furniture, jewelry. Imagine each glory being brought into God's city and offered to him as an act of worship. Think of the greatest achievements of human civilization, freed of the effects of sin, perfected and forever displaying the beauty of God who made us in his image.

While one huge thing will be different—the absence of death, mourning, crying and pain (Rev 21:4)—this world will survive in the age to come. God promised to overturn the curse of the Fall—and God keeps his promises. "No longer will there be any curse," he says (Rev 22:3). The cultural mandate God gave in the beginning (Gen 1:28) will be fulfilled as human society develops for God's glory alone.

What we do in this life can survive in the age to come. So if we have built on the foundation of Jesus Christ with "gold, silver, costly stones"— offered our very best to bring God glory—then those works will remain after judgment (1 Cor 3:12-15). Nothing done in faith—no matter how secular—will have been a waste of time on the day the Lord returns. The ship of this world will rise again, God tells us. So delight in the life God has for you and keep on polishing his brass.

Questions for Discussion

1. What purposes does God have in bringing us suffering? How is this answer different depending on whether or not you believe?

2. What are the five myths about death? Which strikes you most? Why?

3. How can you prepare for your own death?

4. What is the ultimate horizon to which Scripture draws our attention? What events does Scripture describe as taking place around the second coming of Jesus Christ?

5. How do the biblical teachings of justification by faith alone and judgment according to works fit together?

6. How will our resurrected bodies be like the bodies we have now? How will they be different?

7. What does the future hold in store for the earth itself? What implications do you think this might have for how we live our lives in the world now?